Come to the
BANQUET

Come to the
BANQUET

Meditations for the Lord's Table

RICHARD ALLEN BODEY
AND ROBERT LESLIE HOLMES,
EDITORS

Baker Books

A Division of Baker Book House Co
Grand Rapids, Michigan 49516

Published by Baker Books
a division of Baker Book House Company
P.O. Box 6287, Grand Rapids, MI 49516-6287

Printed in the United States of America

Library of Congress Cataloging-in-Publication Data

Come to the Banquet : meditations for the Lord's Table / Richard Allen Bodey
   and Robert Leslie Holmes, editors.
        p.   cm.
   ISBN 0-8010-9057-1 (pbk.)
   1. Communion sermons. 2. Sermons, American. I. Bodey, Richard Allen.
II. Holmes, Robert Leslie, 1945– .
BV4257.5.C66   1998
252'.6—dc21   98-21450

Scripture marked KJV is from the King James Version of the Bible.

Scripture marked NASB is from the NEW AMERICAN STANDARD BIBLE®, copyright © The Lockman Foundation 1960, 1962, 1963, 1968, 1971, 1972, 1973, 1975, 1977, 1995. Used by permission.

Scripture marked NIV is from the HOLY BIBLE, NEW INTERNATIONAL VERSION®. NIV®. Copyright © 1973, 1978, 1984 by International Bible Society. Used by permission of Zondervan Publishing House. All rights reserved.

Scripture marked NKJV is from the New King James Version. Copyright 1979, 1980, 1982 by Thomas Nelson, Inc. Used by permission. All rights reserved.

Scripture marked NRSV is from the New Revised Standard Version of the Bible, copyright 1989 by the Division of Christian Education of the National Council of the Churches of Christ in the USA. Used by permission.

For current information about all releases from Baker Book House, visit our web site:
http://www.bakerbooks.com

Contents

Chapters Arranged according to Seasons of the Year

Chapters Arranged according to Scripture Text

Preface

Near Stroudsburg, Pennsylvania, lies the grave of an unknown but greatly celebrated soldier. His gravestone bears these words: "Abraham Lincoln's substitute." Amidst the anguish and tragedy of America's Civil War, President Lincoln chose to honor this man by naming him as his representative. In so doing, the president made that man a symbol of the fact that each soldier who perished on the battlefields was dying that others might live.

That is the essence of the events surrounding the Lord's Supper. No matter what one's Christian tradition, the elements of this Supper are stark reminders that One died that all might live. Many Christians, of course, believe Communion goes far beyond that; but that is a beginning place where all meet and agree.

After inspiring the British to victory in World War II, Winston Churchill was rejected in his bid for reelection. That defeat was hard to accept, and Churchill, for several months, was uncertain what to do with his future. Asked if he might be persuaded to put his remarkable oratory skills to work as a gospel preacher, Churchill hesitated only a moment before making his reply. "Only a fool," said he, "believes he can address the same crowd week after week with essentially the same message and continue to hold their attention." He quickly added, "I may have lost an election, but I am not a fool!" Churchill may have been right about many things, but the Bible still says, "God was pleased through the foolishness of what was preached to save those who believe" (1 Corinthians 1:21 NIV). Good preaching, however, of the kind to which Churchill alluded when he spoke of holding attention, demands hard work; and preaching a sermon for Communion presents a particular challenge for almost all preachers. That is the motivation behind this book.

This collection of sermons for the Lord's Supper is intended to assist pastors as they prepare for one of their most challenging preaching tasks. If the messages contained in these pages provide kindling to light fires in pastors' hearts and pulpits, that alone will be a wonderful reward for the contributors and the editors of this volume.

We dare to hope for even more than that, however. We hope that laypeople will find these sermons refreshing and encouraging in their personal preparation for coming to the Lord's Table and for their journey in faith.

The contributors to this collection intentionally represent a healthy cross section of denominations. However, a binding thread holds us all together: We all share a love for preaching and a commitment to the "faith that was once for all entrusted to the saints" (Jude 3 NIV). Regardless of the tradition each one follows when it comes to Communion, each contributor holds a high view of Scripture and the great creeds of historical Christianity. Each contributor was granted freedom to choose the Scripture translation he or she preferred. Unless otherwise noted, Scripture quotations throughout each sermon are taken from the version listed under the initial Scripture passage.

The sermons are directed to particular days in the church year and other special days; however, many could be easily adapted for other occasions.

We express our deep appreciation to the contributors for their good work and trust that their patience in waiting is rewarded by seeing this volume published.

Paul Engle, editor of professional books at Baker Books, was especially helpful in the preparation process. Without his wise counsel and words of encouragement along the way, this book never would have seen the light of day. Thank you, Paul.

We are grateful, too, to Betty Chapman of the First Presbyterian Church in Pittsburgh, who typed and retyped many of the manuscripts.

Last, but certainly not least, our wives, Ruth Bodey and Barbara Holmes, are worthy of special recognition for putting up with us and encouraging us throughout this project. In gratitude to God for them, we dedicate this book to their honor.

We now send this volume forth with the prayer that he who made his Table our table will be pleased to use our efforts for his own glory.

Richard Allen Bodey
Robert Leslie Holmes

2 Timothy 4:2

1

Catalog America

WILLIAM L. SELF

> Vanity of vanities, says the Teacher, vanity of vanities! All is vanity.
>
> Ecclesiastes 1:2 NRSV

*I*f your mailbox is like mine, it groans under the burden of catalogs this time of year. Last Saturday's mail delivery was especially loaded with a vast assortment of catalogs covering, it seemed, every need or desire I might possibly ever have.

America's Catalog Consciousness

There are 10,000 companies in America in the mail-order business, and these 10,000 companies mail 13.5 billion catalogs every year. It seems that every one of them arrives at my doorstep.

Fifty-five percent of the adult population in America will make at least one purchase out of a catalog this year, and $51.5 billion will be spent on catalog purchases in our country. That is big business.

The catalogs are precisely defining us, or so the sociologists say. Now, that troubles me a little bit, for I am a catalog-aholic, and I never see anybody in them who looks like me. For example, I have not found one bald person in all these catalogs. I have found only one gray-haired person; she models in the American Express catalog and looks the picture of sophistication. I have not found one overweight or, to be politically correct, corpulently-challenged person in all these catalogs. All their citizens seem to possess the perfect body type and are immaculately coiffured.

Catalogs are part of the American landscape. Americans are using them, the sociologists tell us, primarily because women have gone back into the workforce. We no longer shop recreationally as we once did. Our fascination with catalog shopping is a convenience thing. It is to the department store and the merchandising of America what the video is to the movie theater.

The Orvis, Lands' End, J. Crew, and J. Peterman catalogs all come to my house. I especially like the catalog from Brooks Brothers. Their models always look like they just graduated from Yale, Princeton, or Harvard, or are going to an alumni meeting at one of those schools. I like the American Express catalog too. Its models are different from the others. They are all arranging potpourri with beautiful people around the Christmas tree. They are just exactly as we want to be.

Imagine, if you will for a moment, that each of these catalogs represents a neighborhood. In a sense they do, for they are geared to the people of our various neighborhoods. Come with me to some catalog neighborhoods you may know. If you are honest, you may even find yourself in here. If we go by the Ralph Lauren neighborhood, you may see someone who looks like you. On down the street, turn into the J. Crew neighborhood—you know that catalog, do you not? I have often wanted to move into the J. Crew neighborhood because the people don't seem to be so stuck-up, and they seem unfailingly stylish. They all look as though they go to a yard sale, buy an old piece of furniture, and spend Saturday afternoon, in perfect weather, in perfect clothes, just perfectly rumpled, dabbing paint on the furniture and on each other. All the men have a full head of hair. Indeed, they all look like they have the hair of fifteen-year-olds and the same kind of physique.

14

The people in the J. Crew neighborhood drink mint iced tea they made for their touch football game, which they played after painting furniture. There are no old people, no broken people, no dysfunctional people in that neighborhood. Catalog kids are always beautiful, and they all behave just as they should. Each neighborhood, particularly the J. Crew neighborhood, is populated with the new men: men who are naturally literate in the kitchen, men who change diapers.

Then there is the L. L. Bean neighborhood. I'm not a good fit for the L. L. Bean neighborhood association simply because I don't hunt, camp, or chop my own wood. Have you noticed that in the L. L. Bean neighborhood there are no Nintendos or microwaves? Everything is hand-blocked, hand-sewn, American-made. I am not rumpled perfectly enough to live in this neighborhood. I have noticed that in the J. Crew neighborhood, the Ralph Lauren neighborhood, and the L. L. Bean neighborhood (not the American Express neighborhood), everyone has a four-wheel-drive vehicle. You cannot live there if you don't own a four-wheel-drive. (The folks live on good paved roads, but a four-wheel-drive is a mark of membership.) I have also noted in the L. L. Bean neighborhood that fashion is avoided. Buy it now; wear it forever.

I could go on about all of these catalogs. Orvis is right near L. L. Bean, except that you have to fish a lot to live in Orvis. Lands' End tries to incorporate everything you find in L. L. Bean and Orvis, but they are a little bit more on the utilitarian and middle-class side.

The Catalog Myth

Let's be realistic. All the people who live in these catalogs are perfect. They have perfect neighbors and perfect children. They never dress imperfectly. There is no disease in these neighborhoods, and nobody ever dies. Catalog neighborhoods tell the story of no family problems and no rebellious children. They give the picture of eternal youth and never-ending prosperity. Their corporations never downsize and nobody is ever unemployed; nor is anyone ever over employed. They live the ideal, perfect life. They have never heard of divorce, although I don't find many wedding rings as I look at the J. Crew neighborhood. I guess they just trust each other not to wear one.

Catalog neighborhoods may be the defining mark of America. Perhaps you aspire to live in catalog neighborhoods. They may be the benchmark by which you measure who you think you are or whom you want to be. However, in time we all find out that they can easily echo what the writer of Ecclesiastes said: "Vanity of vanities, all is vanity."

Advent is the time of year when just about every business in America screams for attention with heavy-duty advertising. Few things are more distracting to our spiritual growth than things themselves.

The Communion Neighborhood

We cannot get to the Lord's Table by way of the L. L. Bean neighborhood, the J. Crew neighborhood, or the American Express neighborhood. One reason we cannot come is that this Table demands something no catalog can sell us. This Table is the great leveler of people from all walks of life. At this Table, we are all one: one in need, one in hope, one in poverty of soul, and one in need of a Savior.

It would be an absolute sacrilege to come to this Table and celebrate the broken body and shed blood of the Lord Jesus Christ believing that somehow we got here on our own merit. None of us bringing our perfect lives can enrich this Table. We cannot celebrate our perfection in the face of Christ's brokenness. Such an idea has no place here. He was God in human flesh, and he was broken for each of us. There was real blood in real wounds in his hands, on his forehead, across his back, all for my sake and yours. He suffered pain and loneliness as real as we have ever felt. There was a true sense of being left out of all things when he cried out, "My God, my God, why?"

If I read the Scriptures correctly, we are qualified to come to this Table, not because we have purchased our four-wheel-drive vehicles and driven them through our perfect neighborhoods, perfectly dressed, to come to a perfect church, to sit in perfectly comfortable pews, to celebrate our perfect lives. We are qualified to come because, at least in some small way, we can identify with his broken body. We come here because we know we are not perfect but broken; broken by our own sense of sinfulness and broken by life in a world where we live for the present. We come because we now know that he alone is able to put broken people back together again. No one but Christ can redeem our imperfections, and we all have them.

If there is one among us who does not have scar tissue, who has not cried through the night, who has not wept out of his or her own soul, "My God, my God, why?" then that one is not yet ready to eat and drink here. If you have not yet received the letter, the phone call, or the visit that turned your life into a downward spiral for a while, I assure you, you will. If you live in the perfect neighborhood, you still have life to live. If you have flesh on your bones and blood in your veins, you will be scarred before you leave this world.

So why do we come to this Table? If we don't come because we are good enough, why are we here? Through the years, Christians have been good in drawing a line determining who could come to the Lord's Table and who could not. With reckless abandon, I will show you my line in the sand. You do not need this Table if you are perfect. You do not need this Table if you have not been broken, because you cannot identify with torn flesh and spilled blood. You do not need this Table if your life is lived in Catalog America where nobody ever hurts and no one knows disappointments. It's not too much turkey that puts that sunken look in our eyes. It is torn relationships, broken dreams, and grieving as parents and children that make us ready to come here. That is what makes us human. That is what makes us aware of our need for the Savior.

Christ comes again to this Table and invites you and me to partake of its elements. He knows what makes us cry and what hurts us most of all. He has been through it all in our behalf. God in the flesh. They nailed him. He bled. He died. And, he was resurrected, as we shall also be. Through his brokenness we are made whole again. As Isaiah says, "By his stripes we are healed."

Come to the Lord's Table if you know what it is to be broken. Come to the Lord's Table if you do not fit in the perfect catalog neighborhood. Come to the Lord's Table if there is pain in your life, or if life has not worked out the way you planned it. Come here with honesty enough to admit your pain and anxiety, your disease, depression, and despair. Come here for hope. Come with no money, for what is here is not for sale at any price. Come and eat and drink freely of his grace, for there is a seat here with your name on it.

A native of Winston-Salem, North Carolina, William L. Self is a Southern Baptist. A former president of the Georgia Baptist Convention and of the Foreign Mission Board of the Southern Baptist Convention, he is pastor of the Johns Creek Baptist Church in Alpharetta, Georgia. He was educated at Stetson University and Southeastern Baptist Theological Seminary before earning his doctorate in theology at Emory University. The author of numerous articles and several books, he was appointed Special Ambassador to Liberia by former President Gerald R. Ford.

2

Jesus, Why Did You Come?

GEORGE C. FULLER

> The Son of Man came not to be served but to serve, and to give his life a ransom for many.
>
> Matthew 20:28 NRSV

Suppose for a few minutes that you want to know what Christmas is all about. You are not likely to find a substantial answer to that question at the mall; it's hard enough to find even a parking space there. You want to know the meaning of Christmas; network television is not going to help much. Where can you look? The Bible, of course.

Let's narrow our survey to Jesus himself and ask, "Will you please tell us what Christmas is all about? Jesus, why did you come?" Any full answer must take into account all that Jesus revealed about himself. We cannot now attempt that kind of overview. Suffice it to say, from beginning to end, the Bible sets its focus on the coming of Jesus. Moreover, it seems that Jesus himself understood his coming to be for one purpose: as God's

Son, to be the Savior of his people. His birth and his death, Christmas and Communion; the one points to the other.

Sent for Service

Jesus said much about fulfilling the Father's will by his life and death. Let us look at the one dramatic claim that forms our text: "The Son of Man came not to be served but to serve, and to give his life a ransom for many" (Matthew 20:28).

Our understanding of the setting is broadened by additional details given in Mark 10:35–45. From Matthew and Mark we learn that Jesus had just said he would be condemned to death. He is going to experience mocking, flogging, death by crucifixion, then be raised on the third day.

In that confused moment in the life of Jesus' disciples a mother speaks (see Matthew 20:20). She is the mother of the blood brothers James and John, two of his disciples. There she is, kneeling before Jesus, the way one kneels before a king, and asking him for a favor: "Declare that these two sons of mine will sit, one at your right hand and one at your left, in your kingdom" (Matthew 20:21).

Salome, the mother, showed remarkable faith. She believed that Jesus was worthy of her worship, and further, that he had a kingdom in which he could and would dispense positions of importance. She sensed that the disciples of Jesus would share in that kingdom. Perhaps her sons shared that profound insight with her. If so, all three of them made serious errors in their calculations.

Their basic mistake was that they misunderstood the nature of Jesus' kingdom. They had no idea what it meant, and still means, to be a subject in that kingdom. However firmly entrenched in their minds, and in our minds, these equations, they are all wrong. To be great is to have power. To achieve stature is to have authority over others. You can gain reward without suffering, a crown without a cross. If Salome was the sister of Jesus' mother, Mary, James and John were his first cousins, close kin and close disciples, perhaps friends from childhood; yet even they could make such serious mistakes.

Jesus responded, "You do not know what you are asking. Are you able to drink the cup that I am about to drink?" (Matthew 20:22). A cup, in this context, is what God wills someone to experience. It may be a cup of joy or a cup of sadness. For Jesus, it was soon to be a cup of suffering and pain so severe that he prayed, "My Father, if it is possible, let this cup pass from me; yet not what I want but what you want" (Matthew 26:39). John himself would later record what Jesus said when Peter tried to defend him: "Put your sword back into its sheath. Am I not to drink the cup that the Father has given me?" (John 18:11).

To drink of the cup God gives you is to move willingly, submissively down the path he sets before you. Jesus asked James and John if they were able to follow him to his cross and experience their own suffering and cross in his service.

Their answer was a pledge of allegiance and an affirmation that they would fulfill that pledge: "We are able." Did they have any idea what they were talking about? Perhaps they thought there would be a fight, war, revolution. They were not called the Sons of Thunder for nothing. Self-confidence seems to have been no problem for them. "We are ready to fight, even die, with you, Jesus," their answer asserted.

"You will indeed drink my cup," Jesus told them. At this point, however, they had no idea what that cup would mean for them.

James was the first of the eleven faithful disciples to die, slaughtered by Herod (Acts 12:1–2). John lived the longest among them. He, perhaps, was the only one not martyred. Caring for Mary, Jesus' mother, he was eventually exiled to the Island of Patmos. During that time he was so carefully composing—perhaps out of extended conversations with her—books that are a treasured part of our Bible. William Barclay mentions an ancient Roman coin on which there is the profile of an ox facing an altar and a plough. One is pictured as a sacrifice, the other as a lifelong servant. Underneath that picture are the words *Ready for either.* For James, life was to call for full, early sacrifice; for John, sacrifice of a different order, perhaps even more demanding. Each followed Jesus to the end, throughout life, whether short or long.

How did the other disciples feel when they overheard this conversation? When the ten heard it, they were angry with the

21

two brothers. Misdirected ambition brought strife. Instead of twelve, now they became ten and two; and the ten were angry with the two. Rampant push for donated honor brought jealousy and division. Tragically, that pattern of behavior and reaction has not disappeared in the Christian world.

Jesus called the ten and the two to himself in order to make clear their serious mistake and this radical truth: "You know that the rulers of the Gentiles lord it over them, and their great ones are tyrants over them. It will not be so among you; . . . but whoever wishes to be first among you must be your slave; just as the Son of Man came not to be served but to serve, and to give his life a ransom for many" (Matthew 20:24–28).

In the politics and business of the ancient world, leaders lorded it over those under them. Leaders were often tyrants. Think of a pyramid; imagine that it is the model for life in the world then and now. The object is to—as we say—work your way up that pyramid so that greatness will increase as you near the top. Questions used to determine your greatness, or lack of it, will sound like this: How many people are in your department under you? How many people report to you? How large is your company? How many steps are you removed from the president? These are all pyramid questions. The higher you climb, the greater the number of people who are under you, and the fewer to whom you are responsible. Ultimate greatness is then at the very top of the pyramid, right at the point, the vertex. I am sorry to disappoint all of us, but no one really ever gets there. It seems that everyone ultimately is responsible to someone. Yet, we give our lives to the climb, sometimes hurting others as we struggle to be above others.

For Jesus, service is the measure of greatness. In the world, however, the issue is more often how much service you receive, not how much you give. Happiness and success are assumed to be found at the top of the pyramid, while at the bottom there is only drudgery and misery. Plato said, How can a man be happy when he has to serve someone? For the Greeks, menial service had no dignity, especially as one looked up at the pyramid above him with all its weight, hopelessness, and oppression.

Jesus came to change the system so firmly entrenched in human understanding that it even reached to his own chosen disciples.

He did not make small, subtle changes. He turned the whole thing upside down. The Christian can view life as a pyramid standing on its point, its peak, its vertex. True greatness is to be found in deep commitment to serve others, to work your way down the pyramid. These then are reasonable questions: How many people can I help? How much good can I do? Can I consume less of the service of others, less of their attention? His people need to be redeemed out of the world's pyramid by his gift of a ransom so that they might properly serve him and others.

The path to his right hand and to his left hand is a full contradiction of the world's scheme. No one's life and death make that more clear than Jesus' own. Why did you come, Jesus? His answer: "The Son of Man came not to be served but to serve." By no means did he seek to absorb the service of others. His washing of the disciples' feet is a window into his entire life and death. So, there is finally one answer to the Christmas question. It is not found in the mall nor in the media: Jesus came to serve, not to be served, and indeed to turn the world's system upside down.

A Ransom for Many

Our passage closes with this second reference to the purpose of his coming: "The Son of Man came . . . to give his life a ransom for many" (Matthew 20:28b).

Some kind of ransom is involved in many television programs. Television scriptwriters, however, did not invent the idea. The Old Testament speaks of ransoms. Rabbis at the time of Jesus taught that if a woman was taken captive and a demand was made upon her husband for as much as ten times her value, he must ransom her the first time. Subsequently, however, he ransoms her only if he desires to do so but need not ransom her if he does not wish to do so (*Babylonian Talmud*, Kethuboth 52a).

A ransom is a price paid for a soldier captured by an enemy. Perhaps the ransom involves delivery of an imprisoned criminal for the release of innocent people taken captive. It was the price paid for a slave at the auction block. The slave was ransomed from servitude to one master to become the slave of another, or to become free. Jesus came to pay that kind of penalty, to gain deliverance from bondage, captivity, death.

The text says that he did it for many. We think of the words spoken at the Last Supper: "For this is my blood of the covenant, which is poured out for many" (Matthew 26:28).

At our local library, I made copies of the *New York Times,* dated March 2 through March 5, 1932. Large headlines and long articles tell the story of the kidnapping of Charles Augustus Lindbergh Jr., twenty-month-old son of the famous aviator and his wife. Ransom notes soon came. It never seemed fully clear which ones were genuinely from the kidnapper and which may have been sent simply in hope of receiving a bogus payment. They all called for a ransom. On May 12, the baby's lifeless body was found less than three miles from the Lindbergh home. Although even recent studies question his guilt, Bruno Richard Hauptmann was executed for that crime on April 3, 1936.

How much would you give for the return of a child, especially if that child was your baby? Many of us would say, "everything, at least everything over which I have control. I would give it all to redeem my child. I want my baby back. The cost does not matter!"

Christmas is about a baby given to redeem the world, a baby born to die. The Father spared no price, held back nothing, giving his only Son.

Jesus came to deliver James and John and us from the trap of this world's system. He comes to set us free, so that we may serve him.

Jesus, why did you come? "The Son of Man came not to be served but to serve, and to give his life a ransom for many" (Matthew 20:28).

To understand Christmas you have to see Calvary. As you look at the cradle made of rough wood, you must think of the cross. You hear the voice echoing again and again in your ear, "You shall call his name Jesus, for he shall save his people from their sins." We come to the Communion Table at Christmastime, with understanding, faith, and gratitude for him who was the greatest gift of all.

George C. Fuller was born in Fort Wayne, Indiana. A minister in the Presbyterian Church in America, he has degrees from Haverford College, Princeton Theological Seminary, Babson College, and a Doctor of Theology from Westminster Theological Seminary. In addition to serving as a pastor in Alabama, Maryland, and Minnesota, he was formerly Executive Director of National Presbyterian and Reformed Fellowship and President of Westminster Theological Seminary. He is currently a pastoral minister in Cherry Hill, New Jersey. He is the author of *Play It My Way* (Chicago: Moody Press, 1973).

3

Remember the Stones

Paul David Reynolds

Then Joshua summoned the twelve men from the Israelites, whom he had appointed, one from each tribe. Joshua said to them, "Pass on before the ark of the LORD your God into the middle of the Jordan, and each of you take up a stone on his shoulder, one for each of the tribes of the Israelites, so that this may be a sign among you. When your children ask in time to come, 'What do those stones mean to you?' then you shall tell them that the waters of the Jordan were cut off in front of the ark of the covenant of the LORD. When it crossed over the Jordan, the waters of the Jordan were cut off. So these stones shall be to the Israelites a memorial forever."

Joshua 4:4–7 NRSV

O n the first day of the New Year, resolutions are particularly significant. That is when people begin to live out what they have resolved to accomplish. Resolutions do not just materialize out of nothing. They are the result of reflection, review, remembrance. Like the bloom of a lovely flower, resolutions grow out of the stalk of remembrance.

26

One of the principle words in the Christian vocabulary is *remember.* Throughout the Bible, we are told to remember God's mighty acts for us. There are virtually thousands of references to the believer's remembrance or memory. The biblical memory is not just theoretical; it's not merely the recalling of an objective image. Biblical memory recalls conditions and determines the behavior of the one who remembers. This was true for the ancient Hebrews as well as for God's people today. Memory is an important part of one's belief.

For the ancient Hebrews, the remembrance of the past meant that what was recalled became a present reality, and that present reality controlled the will. In this way, memory revives faith.

Joshua succeeded Moses as the leader of God's chosen people, the Hebrews. After Moses led the people out of the land of bondage in Egypt, God miraculously opened the Red Sea. This afforded the Hebrews their escape from Pharaoh's army. They were then free and ready to enter the Promised Land, Canaan. But they feared the inhabitants of Canaan and failed to receive God's promise. Twelve spies searched out the land. Only two of the twelve trusted God for a victory, Caleb and Joshua. So the Hebrew people were condemned to wander in the desert for forty years.

Then, when they approached the Promised Land the second time, God chose Joshua to lead his people. The Jordan River barred their entry. This was at the time of the rainy season, coupled with the melting of snow in the Lebanon mountains. The Jordan River was swollen at this flooding time. But God again chose to perform a miracle. God opened the river as he had opened the Red Sea so his people could cross over on dry ground.

It was at this time that God gave Joshua instructions to establish a memorial. He was to set up a cairn of twelve stones taken from the dry riverbed. These memorial stones were to serve as a reminder of God's mighty act for his people. Joshua obeyed the Lord, his God, as our Scripture text illustrates. One representative, chosen by Joshua from each of the twelve tribes, selected a stone and carried it on his shoulder to the other side. There the stones were set up as a memorial. When their children and grandchildren would ask later, "What do these stones mean to you?" they were to respond by telling the children of God's mighty act

27

of stopping the waters of the Jordan River so that they could cross over to the Promised Land on dry ground. The memory of those stones would serve as a memorial to the Israelites forever.

This Old Testament memorial is a preview of the New Testament remembrance in the Lord's Supper. For the Christian, the crossing of the Jordan River typifies the believer's death with Christ. So then, the reasons for remembering the stones by the Hebrews are the same for Christians remembering the Lord's death until he comes. Both are the mark of remembrance. Both initiate resolution to better living.

I once read a story of an old man who dreamed about his past. He saw a long list of things in his life for which he was sorry and ashamed. He dreamed he took a sponge and was about to scrub them away. But to his amazement, he found that the deeds of gold shining through the story of his life had been achieved by regret and sorrow over past transgressions. If he wiped away his wrong acts, he would, at the same time, wipe away those deeds of nobility and beauty in his character.

So it is in our own lives. Even our sins and follies, when we repent of them and ask the Lord for forgiveness, can be made stones in the walls of a godly life. At the Lord's Supper we are called to remember for several reasons.

Remember out of Obedience

The first thing God commands of the life of a believer is obedience. Before a person comes to Christ, his or her life is characterized by disobedience. But out of love, God acts to bring the sinner to repentance and faith. When one is born anew by faith, God then insists on obedience. He does so to prepare the believer for living victoriously.

The life of Joshua is an example. Joshua learned to rule God's people first, by obeying; then he was given charge over God's people. He was Moses' personal attendant during his life and the curator of Moses' writings after his death. God set his seal upon Joshua as the successor of Moses. With Joshua's commission and his assumption of command, we find the first miracle in the conquest of Canaan. Joshua was present when Israel miraculously crossed the Red Sea. Now he participates in another supernatural dividing of the waters. And he commemorates God's divine act with a perpetual memorial.

The New Testament Joshua, Jesus of Nazareth, also lived a life of obedience—perfect obedience. In the Garden of Gethsemane, we find the ultimate example of his obedience. As Luke's Gospel tells us: "Then he withdrew from them about a stone's throw, knelt down, and prayed, 'Father, if you are willing, remove this cup from me; yet, not my will but yours be done'" (Luke 22:41–42). And we know that it was God's will for Jesus Christ to suffer and die—for us. The prophet Isaiah had foretold it: "Yet it was the will of the LORD to crush him with pain. When you make his life an offering for sin, he shall see his offspring, and shall prolong his days; through him the will of the LORD shall prosper" (Isaiah 53:10). Jesus Christ obeyed to death, even death on a cross. The night before his death, he instituted the sacrament of remembrance, saying, "This is my body that is for you. Do this in remembrance of me. . . . For as often as you eat this bread and drink the cup, you proclaim the Lord's death until he comes" (1 Corinthians 11:24b, 26). Christians, then, are to remember out of obedience.

Remember for Instruction

Second, we are to remember for instruction. Scripture says, "When your children ask their parents in time to come, 'What do these stones mean?' then you shall let your children know, Israel crossed over the Jordan here on dry ground" (Joshua 4:21–22).

The memorial stones were a perpetual reminder to Israel of God's saving act. They were a source of inspiration and instruction for all posterity. When new generations would arise, they too would grow in the knowledge and grace of God. In the religion of old Israel there was a strong appeal to remember. Each generation's children were schooled in the history of what God had done and what the covenant required. They learned repeatedly for emphasis about God's mighty deed on the edge of the

Jordan in order that they might serve the Lord out of gratitude and reverential awe.

In like manner, the sacrament of the Lord's Supper is for instruction. The sacrament is a sign and seal of the believer's salvation in Christ's death. It is also a perpetual memorial in the sight of our children. When they see us take the elements, they will want to know why and if they can also participate. Then we can instruct them on the meaning and significance of the Lord's Supper. This is a believer's duty as a parent. When we faithfully fulfill this responsibility, it opens up wonderful new vistas of faith for our children.

Remember for Blessing

A third reason for remembrance is for our blessing. To remember God's grace is itself a blessing to a Christian's heart. This remembrance not only rekindles faith, it restores the determination to service. That was the experience of the Hebrews of Joshua's day as they contemplated the memorial stones at Gilgal. Christians have a similar experience as they meditate on Christ's death while receiving the Lord's Supper. By partaking of the elements, the presence of Christ is not only remembered but becomes a real presence through that remembrance. This reality serves to excite our faith and renew our commitment. Remembrance thus becomes revival of our spirit. God works uniquely and miraculously through the elements of Communion to restore and quicken within us our spiritual sensitivity.

Joshua's memorial stones and Christ's cross have a close connection. We, ourselves, before we came to faith, were like stones in the midst of the river, dead in our iniquities. But by the Lord's strong hand we were brought out of the deadness of sin and raised up with Christ. When Joshua, or any other Hebrew, looked upon the memorial stones, he was reminded of God's victory. And when any Christian receives the Lord's Supper, he is reminded of Christ's victory. Then once again he knows the blessing of the resurrection. Christ won the victory over sin and death—he did it for us! This is worthy of perpetual remembrance. It seals upon us and within us Christ's divine act for us. It is the bond and pledge of our communion with him and his church. May the elements of the Lord's Supper bind us to him on this first day of the New Year. And may our remembrance excite us to new avenues of Christian service.

Paul David Reynolds, a son of Atlanta, Georgia, was educated at Georgia State University, Columbia Theological Seminary, and Union Theological Seminary in Virginia, where he earned his doctorate. Presently the pastor of Central Presbyterian Church in Huntsville, Alabama, his previous pastorates were in the Carolinas, Florida, and Georgia.

4

Behold the Lamb!

Donald L. Hamilton

The next day John saw Jesus coming toward him and said, "Look, the Lamb of God, who takes away the sin of the world! This is the one I meant when I said, 'A man who comes after me has surpassed me because he was before me.' I myself did not know him, but the reason I came baptizing with water was that he might be revealed to Israel."

John 1:29–31 NIV

*I*t is barely daybreak when the four begin making their way from home toward an unknown mountain destination. Two are servants; the others are father and son. After traveling three days, the father, seemingly instructed by an unheard voice, spots their specific destination in the distance.

"Wait for us here," the Father instructs the servants. "My son and I will go on alone." So, loaded with the necessary tools and materials, father and son set off for the mountain called Moriah.

The Substitute Lamb

If ever a man's heart could explode from the relentless pressure of mingled fear and faith, surely Abraham's might be close to doing just that. His mind races to recall that Isaac was a son of promise, hinted at by God twenty-five years before his birth and specifically promised fourteen years prior to that miraculous event. What a joy this young son had been to Sarah and himself! Abraham watches with a deep love as his son carries the wood for the offering. Isaac is developing into a fine young man, Abraham thinks. All the while, he tries to ignore his mission.

Meanwhile, the mountain looms ever nearer, and Abraham struggles to think clearly about the reason for their journey. His mind seems muddled, his reasoning powers gone. God had clearly instructed him to take Isaac to this place and to snuff his life out on an altar of stone, wood, and fire.

How can this be? So much depends on Isaac. Not only is the continuation of Abraham's own family on the line, but the very fulfillment of God's covenant to establish a new people and give them a new land seems to be slipping away. All of this depends on Isaac—but now God had said, Kill him!

Isaac too is puzzled. He knows they have wood and fire, but that is not enough for a burnt offering. "Where is the lamb, Father?" he asks (see Genesis 22:7). Abraham hardly knows how to answer but responds that God will provide the lamb. They continue their trek onward.

Fearfully faithful, Abraham walks on. He considers his options and other possibilities: He might plead with God to reconsider or, perish the thought, even disobey God. The instructions, however, were clear, and Abraham trusted God to do the right thing. Besides, Isaac had, in a sense, come forth from death once. Women the age of Sarah do not have life in their wombs, yet Isaac had been conceived and born. Might not God raise Isaac from death again? Abraham can only wonder.

At long last they come to the place of offering. An altar is built. The wood is arranged. Isaac is taken by surprise as his father binds him and places him on the wood. The knife is poised, ready to strike.

After what seems to be an eternity, God speaks to Abraham again: "Abraham! . . . Do not lay a hand on the boy, . . . Do not do anything to him. Now I know that you fear God, because you have not withheld from me your son, your only son" (Genesis 22:11–12).

Abraham is startled. Looking up, he sees—to his utter amazement—a ram caught in a thicket. Abraham's previous word to Isaac has been literally fulfilled. God himself has provided a lamb for that special offering; a substitute lamb to take Isaac's place on the altar. Behold, the substitute Lamb!

The Passover Lamb

Time passes and things change. God is faithful to his promises to Abraham, who now has fathered a new nation. However, while there is numerical strength in this new people, Israel, there is political weakness. They are, in fact, in slavery in Egypt, a land distant from their roots.

At last, God raises up a new leader. He is a deliverer named Moses. At God's prompting, he demands that Pharaoh release the Jews so that they might return to their homeland. Pharaoh scoffs and refuses to let them go. God responds by sending a series of plagues upon the Egyptian people. Still, Pharaoh is unbending.

Finally, Moses delivers a final warning to the Egyptian king. Death will come to every firstborn son in Egyptian families, but the Israelites will be spared. Again, Pharaoh's heart is hardened, and he refuses to listen to this severest of warnings.

God's instructions to Moses are clear. A special meal consisting of meat, bitter herbs, and bread baked without yeast is to be eaten by every Jewish family. The blood of an animal is to be smeared on the door frames of every Jewish household.

That very night, God tells Moses, "I will pass through Egypt and strike down every firstborn—both men and animals—and I will bring judgment on all the gods of Egypt. I am the LORD. The blood will be for a sign for you on the houses where you are; and when I see the blood, I will pass over you. No destructive plague will touch you when I strike Egypt" (Exodus 12:12–13).

The meat to be eaten and the blood to be used must be from a yearling without defect. It is to be a lamb—the Passover lamb.

So it is that while death comes in horrible measure to those who oppose God and his people, deliverance comes to those who by faith obey. From this time on, the Jewish people will celebrate Passover annually, including the eating of the Passover lamb. Behold, the Passover Lamb!

The Sacrificial Lamb

The years roll by, and at long last Abraham's descendants claim Canaan for their own. They build a permanent temple to replace the temporary portable tabernacle. Not coincidentally, this temple is constructed on Mount Moriah.

The Mosaic law is now in force, and feasts and offerings are practiced on a regular basis. This had been commanded to Moses by God, as recorded in Exodus 29. Each morning and evening a priest approaches the altar to present an offering to the Lord.

Centuries later, during the lifetime of Jesus and beyond, the writer to the Hebrews tells us, "Day after day every priest stands and . . . offers the same sacrifices, which can never take away sins" (Hebrews 10:11). At least one of these sacrifices is offered in the morning. Another is offered in the evening. Fourteen centuries after Moses, the instructions of Exodus 29 are still being followed.

The sacrificial animal is always a yearling, a lamb given as a sin offering for the sins of all the people. Behold, the sacrificial Lamb!

The Triumphant Lamb

Still another scene unfolds before us. This one is in our future at a time unknown but a time that will last for all eternity. The apostle John in Revelation describes in graphic detail how God ultimately controls all things. Evil will be defeated and God's plans will not be hindered.

Apart from God the Father, there is one other who can rightly be said to be the focal point of this apocalyptic drama. He is mentioned some twenty-eight times in various ways. He is said to be the Shepherd who will lead God's flock. He guards the Book of Life. His wrath is greatly feared by those who oppose God. Cosmic war is waged against him, but he prevails and God's foes are eternally defeated. He is given the superlative title of King of kings and Lord of lords!

When John is first introduced to this person, the scene is startling. In Revelation 4, John has been ushered into God's throne room. He is doubtless reminded of Isaiah 6, where that prophet saw the Lord lifted up, sitting on a throne, with strange six-winged heavenly creatures hovering overhead singing continual praise. The song continues here: "Holy, holy, holy is the Lord God Almighty, who was, and is, and is to come" (Revelation 4:8).

In the next chapter, John sees a sealed scroll that will reveal things to come. Who can break the seal? No one worthy seems to be present. John weeps in despair until his attention is turned to the One who can and will open it. He is introduced to John as "the Lion of the tribe of Judah, the Root of David" (Revelation 5:5).

When John gazes upon him, however, John sees not a Lion but a Lamb. What a sight! The Lamb looks as if it had been slain. It has seven horns and seven eyes. This is a Lamb like no other. This is the Lamb that takes center stage as the rest of Revelation unfolds.

What are we to make of this? How should we understand it? John understood this kind of visual imagery. It was not entirely new to the devout Jew. He recalled that in the period between the Old and New Testaments, Judas Maccabeus and other defenders of Judaism were called horned lambs. This description was also applied during that same period to David and other Old Testament heroes.

This may be a strange idea for us to grasp. We are used to considering a lamb as meek and helpless. Here, however, we see a Lamb who is not a victim, but a victor—the resurrected, conquering, and victorious Lamb. Behold, the triumphant Lamb!

The Sin-Taking Lamb

We must consider one more scene. It takes place at the beginning of Jesus' earthly ministry. He was baptized by John the Baptist. He suffered through forty days of fasting in the wilderness.

He was tempted by Satan and overcame that testing. Once again he approached John and was introduced to the crowd.

Consider for a moment how John might have introduced him. He might have used any one of numerous titles and been both scripturally correct and understood by the people. He might have used the descriptions of Isaiah 9:6: Wonderful Counselor, Mighty God, Everlasting Father, Prince of Peace. He could have spoken of Jesus as the Son of God or the Son of Man. He could have called him the Servant of the Lord or the Branch. He could have called him the Prophet who is to come; or, he might have even used the specific title of the Anointed One, the Messiah.

John, however, chooses to introduce him differently: "Look, the Lamb of God, who takes away the sin of the world!" (John 1:29). Then for the benefit of the people, John explains further: "This is the one I meant when I said, 'A man who comes after me has surpassed me because he was before me.' I myself did not know him, but the reason I came baptizing with water was that he might be revealed to Israel" (John 1:30–31).

John has the wonderful privilege of introducing Jesus to the Jewish nation and to the world. Of all the possible ways to do this, he chooses the title Lamb of God. This name, pregnant with meaning, indicates substitution, as in the case of Abraham and Isaac. It indicates Passover and God's deliverance. It indicates a sacrificial provision for sin, as seen in the daily temple offerings. It anticipates ultimate triumph for those who oppose the opposers of God. All of these thoughts and more are likely in the minds of John's hearers. Look, the Lamb of God, who takes away the sin of the world.

The multiple implications of this title rivet our attention on the anticipated accomplishment of the Lamb. He came into the world to take away sin. The Table of the Lord reminds us of this. Its elements compel us to recall a cross, which was an altar where anticipation became reality. On that cross the Lamb died as our substitute, a sacrificial provision for our sin. It was on that cross where death was so ruthlessly carried out, where a body was broken and blood spilled, that condemnation and death passed over the believer, and forgiveness and life were achieved. It was from that cross and a borrowed grave that the slain Lamb came forth in certain victory.

Do you see him? Do you see the Lamb? John the Baptist, and all of Holy Scripture, invites you to gaze upon him. Look, the Lamb of God, who takes away the sin of the world!

Look! There he is! There in the shadow of a cross, wearing a crown. He is God's unique provision for our deepest needs and loftiest hopes.

Is there a better way to remember and honor him than to come to his Table? No, for it is a reflection of an altar of substitutionary sacrifice with the elements of a broken body and shed blood. It is the fulfillment of Passover. It is a reminder of the approaching kingdom. So, we do this until he comes again.

"Worthy is the Lamb, who was slain, to receive power and wealth and wisdom and strength and honor and glory and praise!" (Revelation 5:12).

Behold the Lamb!

Donald Lloyd Hamilton, a minister in the Evangelical Free Church, spent his growing up years in Canton, Ohio. After graduating from Malone College and Trinity Evangelical Divinity School, he earned his doctorate at Bethel Theological Seminary. His pastorates were in Pennsylvania, Ohio, and Minnesota. Since 1982, he has been Professor of Homiletics and Ministry Studies at Columbia Biblical Seminary in Columbia, South Carolina.

5

Living Water

CHARLENE S. ALLING

So he came to a Samaritan city called Sychar, near the plot of ground that Jacob had given to his son Joseph. Jacob's well was there, and Jesus, tired out by his journey, was sitting by the well. It was about noon. A Samaritan woman came to draw water, and Jesus said to her, "Give me a drink." (His disciples had gone to the city to buy food.) The Samaritan woman said to him, "How is it that you, a Jew, ask a drink of me, a woman of Samaria?" (Jews do not share things in common with Samaritans.) Jesus answered her, "If you knew the gift of God, and who it is that is saying to you, 'Give me a drink,' you would have asked him, and he would have given you living water." The woman said to him, "Sir, you have no bucket, and the well is deep. Where do you get that living water?" . . . Jesus said to her, "Everyone who drinks of this water will be thirsty again, but those who drink of the water that I will give them will never be thirsty. The water that I will give will become in them a spring of water gushing up to eternal life." The woman said to him, "Sir, give me this water, so that I may never be thirsty or have to keep coming here to draw water."

John 4:5–11, 13–15 NRSV

*T*his has been a terrible decade and millennium for the Holy Land. Terrorism and death, rage and retaliation— ancient and modern hatreds seem to cut loose again and again in a place that claims the heart and soul of three great faiths. The more our modern world rockets toward complexity, the more this holy landscape, contested sacred ground where God himself once trod, remains the same. Canaanites and Crusaders, Samaritans and Saracens all have fought and bloodied this land. Despite that, God and his peace remain a constant offering, and the Living Water that flows from Palestine promises to slake the thirst of the world.

Jacob's Well

A few years ago, eight others and I went as a delegation from Virginia to the Holy Land to meet and pray and talk with Christians who live there. One of our stops was St. Luke's Hospital in Nablus on the West Bank, the birthplace of the PLO and a site of terrible carnage of the Intifada. There are signs of conflict and fear everywhere, with boarded buildings and barricades and a population of children with haunted eyes and adults with wounds that are not always visible. We found a place that knows soul-killing impoverishment and grief. There is more to Nablus than a strangled town and a hospital bereft of medicine. Nablus is the site of Shechem, where Joshua and his people made their great covenant with Yahweh to forsake all other gods, to worship the great I AM alone. It is also the site of Jacob's well.

There the nine of us and others found ourselves at midday— hot, thirsty, tired from a morning at the hospital. An ancient grizzled abuna greeted us, an orthodox holy man in black robes who fills his lonely life with prayer and hard work. Our presence absolutely astonished him. For several years now, Nablus had been and continues to be just too dangerous for visitors. The holy man eagerly gestured us in, and we walked along peaceful stone paths surrounded by a garden of flowers and greens.

Reaching a clearing, we beheld the ruins of a vast Crusader cathedral that started centuries earlier where suddenly, one day eight hundred years ago, the workmen laid down their tools and walked away. It would have been enormous, its great stone vaults reaching to the heavens, but now open sky and eyeless arched windows allow the wind to pass. At the front was a huge stone altar; from it I could look back to the far wall and see bloodred anemones blooming among the ruins.

We ventured into the tiny building at the center housing the well and an ersatz shop, and we gingerly descended the uneven steps groping our way to a little lighted room. It was odd, really—an elaborately decorated interior with a surprisingly tiny well-hole into which we had to believe Jacob at one time dipped his animal skin pouches. After buying a few dusty bottles, we read a passage about Jacob and sang "We Are Climbing Jacob's Ladder"; finally we slaked our thirst from the well's depths. The water was cool and sweet and good, and we retraced our steps back up to the bare, ruined choirs of the empty cathedral shell.

The Living Water

Before the invading Crusaders started a church, however, before there was a ratty souvenir stand, before there was a PLO stronghold, Jesus quietly walked into this holy place and sat down. It was midday and he too was tired and thirsty and alone. From our Gospel lesson, we know he encountered a Gentile woman, a seeming outcast, a woman of sorrows and solitude; she had made her way to the well in the noonday sun to draw water. Later, the disciples were shocked to hear that Jesus had initiated the conversation. In that time and culture, only a foolhardy man would have considered such an action. Others too throughout the centuries have been hard pushed to understand why Jesus would break the taboo of a Jew conversing with a despised Samaritan.

There, nonetheless, they are, through providence—Jesus who is thirsty and the woman with the water. The story unfolds further. Like the inquisitive Pharisee, Nicodemus, or the bewildered disciples, Nathanael and Philip and Thomas, the woman asks lots of questions of the Lord, some naive, some pointed. Determined somehow to get it right, she hoped she would find the right answer.

41

What Is the Answer?

An apocryphal story about the twentieth-century writer Gertrude Stein says that on her deathbed she opened her eyes and asked, "What is the answer?" Then, after a long silence, Gertrude Stein asked, "What is the question?"

The Samaritan woman banters with this seeming prophet about all the fine details of water. She was interested in both the water usually found at Jacob's well and the water of which Jesus spoke. She too is asking, "What is the answer?" Jesus replies in essence, "What is the question?" He shifts the emphasis from the touchable and tangible to the ethereal and eternal. The Living Water he offers cascades from the very Source of life itself and promises everlasting refreshment.

We all thirst for it, every child of God. Is it not so? The psalmist laments, "My soul thirsts for God, for the living God. When shall I come and behold the face of God?" (Psalm 42:2). The prophet Jeremiah too speaks of God as a "fountain of living water" (Jeremiah 17:13). Water is a sign of the Messiah to all in the Holy Land. Jesus, knowing this, speaks in a language even this woman of Sychar, a Samaritan, might understand. It is the language of water.

When she falls back to regroup, she admits that, yes, she believes the Messiah will come, but he will be her Samaritan Messiah, and when he comes, he will explain everything.

Jesus' reply shakes her to her very bones: not when he comes, but he is here. "I am he, the one who is speaking to you." I am. The great I AM. The God who is here and is to come. The God who is now and is forever. She capitulates, just as I suspect you and I would do in the presence of God himself, and drops everything to run to tell the people of her town.

Do We Not Thirst?

My question for all of us is: Do we too not thirst? Are not our lives parched and empty in places? Who here has not known a yearning for the great mystery that is God? The woman of Samaria unwittingly found the Christ, the Living Water, standing before her face-to-face. Does he do any less for us? He stands in our midst this day, every day, with arms outstretched and a promise burned into our beings. He will take our yokes upon his shoulders. He will comfort the heavy-laden and refresh us. He will wipe away every tear from our eyes and give us the cool refreshing water of life. Not later; now!

Wellspring of Life

So it was that we wanderers and searchers from Virginia stood on the holy ground above the well and read aloud the story of the woman and Jesus. We broke bread, shared a cup, and softly sang the words cascading in round after round: "Jesus I adore you, lay my life before you, how I love you."

As we partook of the holy mysteries and raised our eyes and voices to the sky above us, the sweet music floated up. It was borne as prayer-laden incense, borne up through the eyeless windows, beyond the jagged unfinished walls. It was lifted above the broken homes and hearts and dreams of a country without peace, up into the very heart of heaven. What once seemed an empty shell of a forgotten cathedral became a perfectly crafted chalice filled with the stuff of hope. It was transformed into a source of Living Water to slake the thirst of all who believe and a wellspring of life everlasting.

Charlene S. Alling, born in Newport, Rhode Island, is an Episcopal priest. She served previously as a law enforcement chaplain. She earned undergraduate and graduate degrees in psychology and history from the University of Connecticut and a Master's of Divinity from Yale Divinity School, before undertaking postgraduate studies at Claremont Graduate School and Berkeley Divinity School, New Haven, Connecticut. She is presently on the staff of St. Paul's Episcopal Church, Mount Lebanon, Pennsylvania. Her previous publications include poetry in *The Living Church*.

6

Judgment at the Lord's Table

R. T. KENDALL

That is why many among you are weak and sick, and a number of you have fallen asleep. But if we judged ourselves, we would not come under judgment. When we are judged by the Lord, we are being disciplined so that we will not be condemned with the world.

1 Corinthians 11:30–32 NIV

The Lord himself is unusually present at his Supper. I say unusually present, acknowledging his omnipresence. Psalm 139:7–8 says, "Where can I go from your Spirit? Where can I flee from your presence? If I go up to the heavens, you are there; if I make my bed in the depths, you are there." God's presence is everywhere. There are, however, various degrees of his presence. The Lord's Supper is one of those times when the Lord's presence is affirmed most powerfully. He likes us to recognize that. Not to discern his presence at the Supper is to show contempt for his promise to be there.

Paul said, "Whoever eats the bread or drinks the cup of the Lord in an unworthy manner will be guilty of sinning against the body and blood of the Lord" (1 Corinthians 11:27). We, therefore, are guilty of his body and blood as though we personally cru-

44

cified him, which indeed we all did. Our sins nailed him to the cross. When we drink worthily by acknowledging our unworthiness, we are removed from the guilt of having crucified him.

Verse 29 of 1 Corinthians 11 says that anyone who eats and drinks without recognizing the body of the Lord eats and drinks judgment on himself. The Authorized Version says *damnation*, but that is too strong a word. The Greek word means *verdict*, usually in an unfavorable sense. Yet, it is possible that God could overrule, and I think we can all thank him that he has. Many of us have drunk judgment, but he has been gracious to many of us in spite of it.

The word *judgment*, or being judged, is used five times in verses 29 to 34. It demonstrates the inseparable connection between the wrath of God and the cross of Christ. The Lord's Supper mirrors Jesus' death on the cross and what he does for all of us. The fact that judgment can follow unworthy partaking shows how the cross of Christ and judgment are connected inseparably. Romans 5:9 says we have been justified by his blood so that we will be saved from God's wrath through him.

The one who trusts in the Christ who died on the cross will be spared of coming wrath or hell. It is a wonderful thing to know that we are not going to hell. Because there is a hell, God sent his Son to die on a cross for our sins. It is his blood that justifies us, that saves us from the coming wrath.

Nevertheless, the Christian who partakes unworthily may get just a taste of wrath, what the Bible calls chastening, or being disciplined. This is the meaning for the word in verse 32 of 1 Corinthians 11: "When we are judged by the Lord, we are being disciplined so that we will not be condemned with the world." How is the world condemned? By being sent to hell. While Christians will not go to hell, when we drink unworthily, we are setting ourselves up for being disciplined.

There are three things to be seen here.

The Presence of Judgment

"That is why many among you are weak and sick, and a number of you have fallen asleep." This is the explanation of a fact that nobody present at the time denied. In the church at Corinth were people who were weak and sickly, and many had died. What does it mean to say many were weak? It probably refers to a physical state, because the Greek words for *weak* and *sick* are often used interchangeably. It could also refer to a weak spiritual state. Could it be that the way God has judged many of us is not so much with physical illness, or taking people home prematurely, but that we are in a weak spiritual state? Could it be that our inability to go very far into God's Word with insight and knowledge of his power is because for years our partaking of the Lord's Supper has been a case of drinking judgment upon ourselves? Consequently, we are weak spiritually?

I have often wondered why there is apparently no judgment today. My own explanation is that it is partly because we are not in a revival situation. I could not prove that. It is only my theory. Yet, I wonder, could this weakness refer to a spiritual state? The Greek word can describe a weak conscience, for example. So, it may also refer to a spiritual weakness. If my theory is correct, looking forward to the Lord's Supper with eagerness to discern Christ's body may mean that we are growing in our life with Christ.

Second, Paul writes that many are sick. There is no doubt about his meaning here. He is referring to illness or disease that had broken out. Now, I think a caution is in order: This is not to say that all sickness today is for this reason. Still, it is a fact that in the Bible there were times when there was a connection. Jews often thought in those terms. This is why they came to Jesus asking, "Why is this person ill—was it his sin or his parents'?"

That idea is also seen in James 5, where we have the anointing with oil: The prayer offered in faith will make the sick person well; the Lord will raise him up. *If he has sinned,* he will be forgiven. It means that in an illness brought on by sin, the sin can be forgiven. Remember, it says, *if* he has sinned . . . showing that the sickness is not necessarily the result of sin. The last thing the Lord would have anybody believe today is that all illness is because of God's judgment. In truth, all of us have been dealt with in mercy. Yet we know that in the case at Corinth, Paul, speaking prophetically, has just explained to them, "Here's why you have those illnesses, this is why there is that weakness, and this is why many die."

Third, Paul writes of those fallen asleep. That is a euphemism for being dead. Paul reserves this terminology for the death of Christians. For example, in 1 Corinthians 15:6, he says Christ appeared to more than five hundred people at the same time. Most of these, Paul says, "are still living, though some have fallen asleep." In a similar vein, 1 Thessalonians 4 speaks of those who are asleep in Jesus (v. 14). Jesus also uses this expression, for example, in verse 11 of John 11: "Our friend Lazarus has fallen asleep." Next, Jesus turns around and says that he is dead and that is what he meant when he said "asleep."

What does it mean? It means that some went on to glory as though God said, "Your time is up. Enough is enough." We might say someone died before his or her time. It corresponds to 1 Corinthians 3:15, where Paul talks about works being burnt up and the person himself suffering loss but being saved as though by fire. It was an awesome thing. Some were taken on to glory. It is a serious matter to die before your time. Yet it is wrong to conclude that those who die young are necessarily being judged. Robert Murray McCheyne was twenty-nine years old, a godly man; David Brainerd, who, had he lived, would have been Jonathan Edwards's son-in-law, was twenty-nine. John Calvin was fifty-five. My mother was forty-three, a godly woman.

What we do know about the situation in Corinth is that God stepped in. Peter put it like this: "It is time for judgment to begin with the family of God; and if it begins with us, what will the outcome be for those who do not obey the gospel of God?" (1 Peter 4:17). So, the presence of judgment was there in Corinth. They had abused the Lord's Supper, and Paul said, "That is why many among you are weak and sick."

The Prevention of Judgment

"If we judged ourselves, we would not come under judgment." Thank God he said this. This means if we judge ourselves, God will not have to judge us. What does it mean to judge ourselves? The answer is back in 1 Corinthians 11:28. "A man ought to examine himself before he eats of the bread and drinks of the cup." When I come to the Lord's Supper, I must be sure of three things.

1. *That I have not humiliated the poor.* In 1 Corinthians 11:22, Paul says, "Don't you have homes to eat and drink in? Or do you despise the church of God and humiliate those who have nothing? What shall I say to you? Shall I praise you for this? Certainly not!"

2. *That I affirm those who partake of the Lord's Supper with me.* Now, partly this means discerning the body of Christ, that is, the church, so that I exclude no one and I accept those who are there.

3. *That I affirm the Lord's own promise to be present.* "I tell you, I will not drink of this fruit of the vine from now on until that day when I drink it anew with you in my Father's kingdom" (Matthew 26:29). Christ is present, whether I recognize his presence or not. As Christians, we want to discern his presence at the Supper; John Calvin states it, "As though he were set before my very eyes."

In Psalm 139:23–24 we read: "Search me, O God, and know my heart; test me and know my anxious thoughts. See if there is any offensive way in me, and lead me in the way everlasting." There is nothing to be afraid of when God is present when we have judged ourselves—that is, if we have acknowledged our sin problem—then God's presence is for our good.

The Purpose of Judgment

"When we are judged by the Lord, we are being disciplined so that we will not be condemned with the world" (1 Corinthians 11:32). Painful though his disciplining is, it is wonderful to know that we are not going to hell. In the Greek, the word means *enforced learning.* In other words, if we don't learn voluntarily, God has a way of teaching us a lesson.

The judgment that came on Corinth was temporal judgment, as opposed to eternal judgment. Similarly, if God judges us, we are really being disciplined more than judged. It is temporal judgment, a judgment of grace. It's a marvelous thing when God dignifies you with his discipline. If you do not know what it is for God to discipline you, you have not really been born of the Spirit. None of us is exempt from this. It is a wonderful thing to know that God deals with us graciously, even when he disciplines in judgment.

Scripture speaks of three levels of God's chastening, or discipline:

Plan A—Internal Chastening

That is what Paul was doing in writing this letter. The word that is sharper than a two-edged sword pierces our hearts. God deals with us right here—nobody knows it is happening except us. If God is disciplining you at this moment, that is the best way to have your problems solved. If you can come to the place that he puts his finger on something, and you can say, "Thank you, Lord, for loving me this much," you are judging yourself. That is what I call a Plan A judgment.

Plan B—External Chastening

You are being disciplined. Some of you are weak; some are sick. Exodus 15:26 mirrors this: "If you listen carefully to the voice of the LORD your God and do what is right in his eyes, if you pay attention to his commands and keep all his decrees, I will not bring on you any of the diseases I brought on the Egyptians, for I am the LORD, who heals you."

Jonah ran from the Lord, and God chastened him. He was not weak or sick. Plan B meant being swallowed by the fish. Had Jonah not surrendered to God's will the second time, God had another plan.

Plan C—Terminal Chastening

Paul writes, "A number of you have fallen asleep." Do you know what it is to be terminally chastened by the Lord? It is to have your life taken away. When that happens, we bear the responsibilities for we have been twice warned. Psalm 103:8 says, "The LORD is . . . gracious, slow to anger." It takes a lot to make him angry. When he gets angry, it is awful. Yet David goes on to say, "He does not treat us as our sins deserve or repay us according to our iniquities" (Psalm 103:10). The evidence of it is seen on Calvary's cross and brought to our attention again at the Lord's Table.

> Who is a pardoning God like thee,
> Or, who has grace so rich and free?

R. T. Kendall, a son of Ashland, Kentucky, has been the minister of Westminster Chapel in London, England, since 1977. A Southern Baptist, widely published on both sides of the Atlantic, he is the author of seventeen books, including *Stand Up and Be Counted* (Grand Rapids: Zondervan, 1984). A graduate of Southern Baptist Theological Seminary and the University of Louisville, he earned his Ph.D. at Oxford University.

7

Singing the Scared Away

H. BEECHER HICKS JR.

When they had sung an hymn, they went out into the mount of Olives.

Matthew 26:30 KJV

There is a sense in which all of us are the products of the events and experiences of our childhood. Through them we learn to hope and to dream, to imagine and to make believe, to wonder and to ask questions of the world that surrounds us. Strangely enough, no matter how old we become, no matter how sure and settled our years, there is always deep within us the child who is the product of the past.

There is an experience, common to all our childhoods, that most of us will be unable to deny. Every child who was ever left alone knows what it is to be afraid of the dark. Many a child has come to tears when the final good nights are heard and the bedroom door creaks to a close.

In the dark, strange shadows make their way across the ceiling and pose themselves in peculiar places along the walls.

51

In the dark, sounds one has never heard before become thunderous in our ears; the natural creaks and cracks of the house seem louder somehow.

In the dark, a child is immobilized and terrorized by things that go bump in the night.

You and I may have night-lights on our walls, or we may leave a light on in the hall. It is because we are the products of our childhood, and every child knows what it is to be afraid of the dark.

I have discovered through the observation of my own children that there is a way to handle this fear of the dark. Throughout her childhood, my daughter was quite fond of an old record player that remains in her closet of childhood memories. In the dark, the record player offered melodies for the night. It did not matter that the record's grooves were worn by time, nor that the sounds came from an oversized bird with outrageously yellow feathers whose name is Big Bird.

As the record played, as the bird sang, as the music played on and on, something happened: Fear was no longer there. When the record sang, she began to sing too. What she was really doing was singing the scared away.

A Time to Be Scared

Ours is a moment in history when the familiar structures that once held the world together are disintegrating before our very eyes. All about us are the unmistakable signs of cataclysmic change.

There is a war raging in the alleys of the Americas—that war of drugs and substance abuse. It corrupts and terrorizes and paralyzes this nation. Our government can pass no laws to destroy it. Even international law is unable to stop it. Children on drugs will steal from their mothers and kill their fathers and never look back. It is dangerous to walk the streets. It is time to be scared.

Our families are disintegrating. Schools are no longer able to adequately educate our children. The church is no longer able to set the moral agenda for the nation. In the words of DeLawd in *Green Pastures,* everything fastened down is busting loose. It is time to be scared.

I recall hearing Martin Luther King Jr. say, "The ultimate measure of a man is not where he stands in moments of comfort and convenience but where he stands at times of challenge and controversy."

We cannot escape it. The night is upon us. The dark surrounds us. It is hard to see any light that will help us make it through. We are hearing voices we have not heard before. Our spirits are unsettled. Our minds are confused. Doubt has nearly defeated us. Anxiety has us tied up in knots. The frightening events of every day wake us up in the morning and put us to bed at night. Every one of us has justifiable reasons to be scared.

Against this backdrop of the terrifying events of human history, I began to search God's Word for direction and guidance. I discovered a word that only Mark and Matthew share. Let me set the stage.

Jesus had come now to the close of his ministry. For three short but eventful years he had made his way across the Judean foothills, around the Sea of Galilee, northward to Tyre and Sidon and the rest. For three years he healed the brokenhearted, delivered captives, gave sight to the blind, and preached the gospel to the poor. Now the end was nearly upon him. Luke says it poignantly and well: ". . . when the time was come that he should be received up, he steadfastly set his face to go to Jerusalem" (Luke 9:51).

It was a Thursday night, and the table was set. Jesus and his disciples gathered to share a final Passover meal. There was nothing fancy about it. It was hardly even a typical, traditional Jewish Seder. All they had—these penniless preachers—was some unleavened bread and enough wine so that each could sip from one cup.

When the Supper was over, when the last prayer stilled in silence and the benediction was pronounced, while Peter pretended nothing would change and John Mark tried to hide his face as he wiped his tears away, they sang a hymn and went out into the Mount of Olives.

Whatever else we might say about the disciples of Jesus, at this point in their history they were scared. These handpicked companions of the Savior were frightened. These who had been trained at his hand, heard his message on the mountain, were there when he calmed the sea, on this night, as they left the Upper Room on the way to the Garden of Gethsemane, were terrified. They had good reason to be. Not only did it appear that the church would die, it also appeared certain that Jesus himself would die. They just did not understand Jesus and this death factor. He kept on talking about volunteering to die and planning to rise. They heard him say, "No man taketh [my life] from me, but I lay it down of myself. I have power to lay it down, and I have power to take it again" (John 10:18).

These disciples were scared. All of their dreams and hopes would be fulfilled in him. Even the nation would be restored to a posture of power through him. The disciples were scared not only because they thought the church would die if Jesus died, they were scared as well because they had just learned around the table that the church, if it lived, would have to live out its ministry in the presence of a traitor.

Perhaps they were all the more scared because they recognized that each of them had traitor traits in their personality. The Bible says that when Jesus brought up the traitor issue, the disciples began to question among themselves, Lord, is it I? They saw Judas when he left, but they still understood that every one of them had the capacity to be treacherous. Don't look now, but the church is still dealing with the traitor problem.

Beyond all of this, however, is the reality that the disciples were scared because they believed that, like Jesus, they would die also. Simon Peter was the one who said he was ready to lay down his life; and it was Thomas who got carted away when he said, "Let us also go, that we may die with him." However, when dying time came around, Peter cursed in Caiaphas's courtyard, and Thomas was so frightened he would not even show up for prayer meeting.

These were the disciples of Jesus! These unbelieving, wishy-washy, doubting, denying, spineless, treacherous, lying, powerless excuses for disciples were all the help Jesus had. The reality is that when they met for a final time over the Holy Supper in that Upper Room, they were scared. That is what drew me to what Matthew said: ". . . and when they had sung an hymn, they went out!"

Implicit in the behavior of the disciples is the answer for how to handle the scary circumstances of life. Properly understood, the task of the church is always to go out.

There is comfort and security staying on the inside, but the task of the church is to go out. Carpeted sanctuaries provide a protected environment for weak and cowardly Christians, but the task of the church is to go out. The church is the church not when it is gathered but when it is scattered, and that is why the task of the church is to go out.

When the time came to leave that Upper Room, no doubt the disciples were hesitant. Christian commitment always marches by the commandment to go! If you are going to be a disciple for Jesus, there is danger in your destiny, but go! You may be required to offer up your body as a living sacrifice, but go! There is no place for cowardly soldiers here, so go! Go through distress, through disappointment, through depression, through the storm, through the wind, through the rain, through adversity, through hard trials, through death itself. Whatever the cost, whatever it takes—go! Listen! Look at this word.

Whenever you come into the presence of Jesus, you never go out the same way you came in. When those disciples came into that Upper Room, their fellowship was already fractured. They had been arguing over seating arrangements at the table. When they arrived for the church service, they were arguing when they came in the door about who would wash whose feet. When they sat down at the table, they could not eat the meal simply because they had been arguing about the political socioeconomic climate and whether Jesus ought to get out of town before it was too late.

There is something extraordinary about being in the presence of Jesus. Whenever you are in his presence,

walls are broken down,
the divided are united,
yokes are broken,
the bound are set free,
captives are liberated,
and the world can't do you no harm!

That is what happens in the presence of Jesus. You never go out the same way you came in.

If you came in broken, you'll go out whole.
If you came in bruised, you'll go out blessed.
If you came in with your head hung down, you'll
    go out with your head held high.
If you came in limping, you'll go out leaping.
If you came in doubting, you'll go out believing.
If you came in through the valley, you'll
    go out to the mountains.
If you came in defeated, you'll go out victorious.

Those disciples came in sad, but they went out singing! They came in separated from each other, but they went out singing together. Those disciples were not just frightened. They were intimidated and terrified, petrified and panic-stricken; yet they went out singing.

As I analyze what happens to a child who is afraid of the dark, it occurs to me that the child is victimized by things that are not there. If the truth be known, the things that most of us are afraid of and intimidated by really are not there—the figments of our own imagination.

The presence of fear in your life is indicative of a faith problem. When we are frightened, it is because the devil induces us to put the emphasis on the wrong reality.

We magnify our sorrow instead of the Savior.
We spend our time on the pain and never on the Provider.
We are paralyzed by pitfalls and never rely on the Promises.
We spend our time in the shadows and never consult the
    Shepherd.
We reduce life to the darkness of night and forget about the
    Bright and Morning Star.

Sometimes you have to forget about the things that frighten, step fearlessly into the night, give no thought to the shadows, and sing the scared away.

Does it surprise you that these disciples decided to sing? It ought not to. Everybody has a time when they need to sing the scared away. When it comes for us, let us not be heard singing the mindless, senseless music of fear. We must sing the songs of our faith. We must not sing the songs of a corrupted culture that would deceive us and keep us from facing the reality of our days. We must sing the songs that our fathers and mothers sang.

I think about how scared they must have been when faced with the lashing whips of the slave master, yet they did not give up; they sang a hymn: "Walk togedder, chillun; don't cha get weary."

Those who fought for my freedom and yours, even when chased by bloodhounds and in spite of tar and feathers, did not fail to face the enemy with courage and determination; and in the process they sang a hymn: "I'm gonna tell God how you treated me when I lay my burden down."

When you prepare your heart by faith and come to the Lord's holy Table, when you eat this bread and drink this cup, then you can go back into a world that gives you plenty of reason to be scared. Go not frightened, my beloved. Go out singing the songs of Zion. Let nothing scare you now that he is in you. "Ye are of God, little children, . . . because greater is he that is in you, than he that is in the world" (1 John 4:4).

H. Beecher Hicks Jr., senior minister of Metropolitan Baptist Church in Washington, D.C., is the author of *Preaching through a Storm* (Grand Rapids: Zondervan, 1987) and *Correspondence with a Cripple from Tarsus* (Grand Rapids: Zondervan, 1990). An honor graduate of the University of Arkansas at Pine Bluff and a recipient of the Rockefeller Protestant Fellowship, he earned his doctorate at Colgate Rochester Divinity School and did postgraduate study at Harvard Divinity School. In 1993 *Ebony Magazine* named him one of America's fifteen greatest African-American preachers. His previous pastorates were in New York, Pennsylvania, and Texas. Dr. Hicks is also president of Kerygma Associates, Inc., a church management consulting firm.

8

This Is My Body; This Is My Blood

JOHN H. DENNIS

When he had given thanks, he brake it, and said, Take, eat: this is my body, which is broken for you: this do in remembrance of me. After the same manner also he took the cup, when he had supped, saying, This cup is the new testament in my blood: this do ye, as oft as ye drink it, in remembrance of me.

1 Corinthians 11:24–25 KJV

Let us return to a Thursday evening, the fourteenth of Nisan, according to Jewish timing. The Passover lamb had been killed during the afternoon. The Feast of Passover was ready. It was after sunset and the streets were dark as Jesus arrived in the Upper Room. He knew that his mission for the salvation of the world was about to be completed. Within hours, he would die by the most cruel death known at the time. Nevertheless, even these last hours Jesus did not keep for himself. He ate the Passover meal and then, for the sake of his disciples, instituted the Lord's Supper.

The devil was busy, as he always is, sowing seeds of discord among the people. He is still very busy among the believers in God. The ceremonial foot-washing took place. Jesus girded himself with a towel. Before the disciples had time to realize what he was doing, he began to wash their feet. Normally, a slave or a servant did this. Once again, Christ demonstrated that he was such a one. "He that is greatest among you shall be your servant" (Matthew 23:11). There is an eternal life principle we all must learn.

After the meal, Jesus took the remaining unleavened bread and the fermented grape juice, now named wine, and said, "This is my body. This is my blood. This do in remembrance of me."

The disciples and Jesus sang a hymn, and he went out to the Mount of Olives very quickly. The intrigue and the planning of Judas and the religious leaders of the day ensued.

This Maundy Thursday, we want to look at the Lord's Supper and take into consideration all of the ramifications of its meaning. To begin with, we take the words of Jesus, "This is my body. This is my blood."

Recently, I made a new will. Since my circumstances had changed, my old will needed to be updated. I made the changes in no uncertain terms. My lawyer did not reinterpret what I said and give it a different meaning. He simply wrote down what I said and will, one day, when I pass away, carry out my wishes. Similarly, Matthew, Mark, and Luke simply wrote down what Jesus said at the Last Supper.

Later on, St. Paul, by inspiration of God, wrote down the words in order that we would remember exactly what our Lord said. Jesus said what he wanted to say. We do not tell him what he did not say.

Jesus made his last will. He bequeathed unto us this precious sacrament. It is to be observed until he comes again. We are not allowed to tamper with a person's last will. The purpose of writing a will is to have one's final wishes carried out.

We believe that when we receive the bread and the wine, we receive the body and blood of Jesus. Why is this? Simply because Christ says so.

I have heard people say Communion is just a memorial time and nothing more. When we serve the Lord's Supper, we do it in memory of Christ. When do we hold a memorial service? We hold it when one is dead. But, if that be true, this cannot be only a memorial, for Jesus is alive. He is risen from the dead. He is alive forevermore.

The "in memory of" is not in memory of Jesus. Jesus is alive. It is in memory of the fact that he died for us! We praise God, however, that he also arose for us.

Let us go to the words of the inspired St. Paul. Paul also received of the Lord, as he so succinctly says, that on the night of Christ's betrayal, he took the bread and wine. By means of such earthly elements, the Lord of life gave us this blessed sacrament.

We also know that if we eat and drink unworthily, we sin against Christ and the body of believers. One thing is certain: We do not sin against bread and wine but against the body and blood of Jesus. How can we sin against something that is not there?

The church traditionally has guarded the Lord's Supper. In some traditions, this is called fencing the Table. Those words carry the image of someone erecting a fence around the Table to protect it from those who are not in communion with the Lord and his church. However, that fence works two ways in that it also protects one who should not come. Scripture speaks a firm word of prohibition for those who eat and drink at this Table in an unworthy manner. Those who come must know what they are doing upon the basis of what God is teaching. They are also to repent of all sin, have love and charity in their hearts, and receive the sacrament with spiritual joy.

I have long appreciated the caution of 1 Corinthians 11:28 and 29: "Let a man examine himself, and so let him eat of that bread, and drink of that cup. For he that eateth and drinketh unworthily, eateth and drinketh damnation to himself, not discerning the Lord's body."

We have a confessional service before we receive Communion. At that time, we ask God to take away our sins and to give us newness of life. We must never come to Communion with unconfessed sin or hate or malice in our hearts. We come to Holy Communion with newness and hope and great assurance that Jesus loves us. This we know, for the Bible tells us so.

When I am hungry, I do not want to see a picture of food, for that may only make things worse; I want to see and feel and taste the food. When I long for a friend, I want to see more than his or her picture. I want to see my friend.

When I truly want to know Jesus, I can know him through his Word. In addition, he has given us a sacrament, Holy Communion; when I receive the bread and the wine, I know that he is with me and I am with him. Come to the altar. Receive Jesus in the sacrament. Amen.

John H. Dennis was born in Marion, Ohio. He is a graduate of Capital University, Columbus, Ohio, with an A.B. degree and of the Evangelical Lutheran Theological Seminary, now called Trinity Seminary, of Columbus, Ohio, with a B.D. degree. He has been the pastor of the Ruthfred Evangelical Lutheran Church, Bethel Park, Pennsylvania, for forty-seven years.

9

Oh, Say! Can You See by the Dawn's Early Light?

ROBERT LESLIE HOLMES

Early on the first day of the week, while it was still dark, Mary Magdalene came to the tomb and saw that the stone had been removed from the tomb. So she ran and went to Simon Peter and the other disciple, the one whom Jesus loved, and said to them, "They have taken the Lord out of the tomb, and we do not know where they have laid him." Then Peter and the other disciple set out and went toward the tomb. The two were running together, but the other disciple outran Peter and reached the tomb first. He bent down to look in and saw the linen wrappings lying there, but he did not go in. Then Simon Peter came, following him, and went into the tomb. He saw the linen wrappings lying there, and the cloth that had been on Jesus' head, not lying with the linen wrappings but rolled up in a place by itself. Then the other disciple, who reached the tomb first, also went in, and he saw and believed.

John 20:1–8 NRSV

*I*t was June 18, 1815. The French, under Napoleon Bona-
parte's direction, were at war with the English, Dutch, and
Germans, commanded by the Dublin-born Duke of Wellington near Waterloo on the Franco-Belgian border. There was
no CNN, no e-mail; there were no satellites. Day after day a sail-
ing ship made the twenty-two-mile sea crossing over the English Channel from France to the south coast of England carrying the latest battlefield news. From there that news was relayed
to London where it was publicly displayed in headline words
spread across the top of the high tower at Winchester Cathedral.

On this fateful day, Londoners read the huge letters placed side
by side that spelled tyranny to their souls: "W-E-L-L-I-N-G-
T-O-N D-E-F-E-A-T-E-D." A heavy fog made the letters
almost impossible to read, but the message they sent was clear.
That fog atop the cathedral tower was compounded in a short
time by another fog, a hard pressing haze that gripped the hearts
of citizens all across London. They knew their future would be
different under Napoleon. The "Little Corporal" as they called
him, mocking his short stature, was regarded a monster by all
loyal subjects of England's king. A future under Napoleon was
not a future they anticipated with joy.

Then something happened that changed everything. Without warning, the wind changed direction, and the fog atop Winchester Cathedral lifted to reveal the message in its entirety for
the first time. It did say "WELLINGTON DEFEATED," but
that was not all it said. The whole message was "WELLING-
TON DEFEATED NAPOLEON AT WATERLOO!" Woe
turned to exultation; defeat became dancing in the streets when
Napoleon "met his Waterloo."

When Jesus Christ died on Calvary's cross, hope died in the
hearts of the gospel's staunchest allies. When the crucifixion fog
lifted, however, it took sadness, defeat, and death with it for all
time. If you stick with the English translations, the full force of
the Greek text gets lost somehow. Three precise Greek verbs
translated with one English word tell the rest of the story.

Cursory Sight

"Mary Magdalene came to the tomb and saw that the stone had been removed from the tomb." The Greek verb *blepo* indicates the level at which Mary observed the tomb that morning and at which many people see life. With a quick glance, Mary saw that the gravestone over the tomb where Jesus' body was laid late on Friday afternoon was no longer in place. As a result of her haste of perception, Mary drew conclusions that were dead wrong. Moreover, the Bible says John, whom "Jesus loved," at first accepted Mary's conclusions at face value.

"Body snatchers!" they declared. Perhaps their misperceptions fed off each other, each of them through doubt reinforcing the other's inaccurate conclusion.

Many of us will remember that July 1996 night when TWA's flight 800 from New York to Paris crashed as a ball of fire into Long Island Sound. For days afterward, the media was filled with bomb stories. At first glance it looked as though an explosive device may indeed have been smuggled on board the airliner. Some of us even "knew" who did it and were ready to go to war. However, on the first anniversary of the explosion, the FBI announced their research had concluded beyond any doubt that there was no bomb. When we look too quickly, we are apt to reach wrong conclusions, which can lead us in the wrong direction.

Critical Sight

"Simon Peter . . . went into the tomb. He saw the linen wrappings lying there. And the cloth that had been on Jesus' head, not lying with the linen wrappings but rolled up in a place by itself." Peter stepped inside the tomb door. The big fisherman was no man's doppelganger. He would reach no conclusions until he analyzed the situation for himself. "He saw the linen. . . ." The Greek verb now is *theoreo*, the root of our English word *theory*, or the verb *theorize*. It means to look judiciously, discerningly, intensely, considerately, shrewdly. Peter theorized within himself. He scrutinized the situation without comment or commitment.

The memory of that rooster sounding reveille a day or two before had not been erased from Peter's conscience. No longer would impulse lead him to hastily made, wrong conclusions. Peter thought about it. His closer, lingering look convinced him there was more to the situation than Mary was seeing. Perhaps he theorized about the gravestone, not only rolled away from the grave but lifted away completely. Lifting a stone that size was a gargantuan task. It would have easily required more than one man to raise a stone like that.

Peter also observed undisturbed body wrappings. Did you ever try to get out of bed without disturbing the bedclothes? The grave clothes Peter saw were undisturbed. The shroud was shaped as though it contained a body, but it was empty like a used cocoon. It looked as though the body had simply evaporated. Then there was that head cloth neatly folded and set aside. No grave robber could remove a body without disturbing its wrappings. No body snatcher ever took time to fold a head cloth. Grave robbers moved with haste and left everything they did not take in disarray. Peter observed it all judiciously. He theorized but offered no answers.

Comprehensive Sight

"Then the other disciple, who reached the tomb first, also went in, and he saw and believed." John, who first accepted Mary's conclusion, stepped in beside Peter and looked again. The Greek verb now is *eido*, from which our English word *idea* is derived. It is more often translated "to know" and related to knowledge. Unlike *ginosko*, meaning acquired knowledge, *eido* is perceptive understanding or insight. The source of *eido* is another Greek word, *horao*, meaning to be enlightened by something for the first time, such as a new idea. We all have had that experience where we looked at a situation differently and a light came on within us. That was what happened to John when he looked again.

Gloom's fog lifted and John understood: This was not the work of a grave robber, but the Grave-beater, Jesus. Satan met his Waterloo at Calvary's cross. John could see that death's hold was gone forever for the whole human race. He quickly calculated that all one needed to do to avoid dying was to believe in the risen, living Lord. In short, he saw God's big idea for sin's remedy and committed the rest of his life to telling it. There is a knowledge that is better than rote learning, a sight beyond merely seeing.

I understand that, in an *eido* way. Growing up in the church, I somehow missed the message of grace. It was not that it was not preached but that I did not hear it in the ears of my heart until I was twenty-two years of age. Until that moment, I reckoned that sin was probably counterbalanced by good works in heaven's economy, and I tried a dozen times or more to "be good." Each time I tried, my own failures ended up frustrating me more than the time before. Then one day I heard about God's amazing redemption through Calvary's cross. It was a wonder of wonders. A light came on inside my soul. The news was so good that at first I thought I had misunderstood the message. When I investigated the Bible, the message of grace took root in this sinner's heart. It so gripped my soul that it revolutionized the whole direction of my life. Instead of aspiring to be a powerful and wealthy businessman, I felt compelled to tell what I had learned about God's love in Christ to everybody in the world. The wonder of that moment when God's light went on inside me still amazes me.

Have you felt the Light of life ignite within your soul? How do you see life? Cursorily, with Mary's hasty look that seems more ready to believe bad news than good? Critically, with Peter's caution that is ever searching but hesitating to make a declaration of commitment? Comprehensively, through the eyes of faith that find the redeemable through Jesus Christ, God's Son, in every negative situation? Bathe your eyes today in the fog-removing wind of the Spirit. See beyond the moment. Something happened inside that tomb that changes everything, everything on this planet forevermore. Jesus is alive! Death and doubt have met their Waterloo!

You will never understand this, however, with a cheap quick glance and a hastily drawn conclusion. To see it, you must step in all the way with Jesus.

Oh, Say! Can You See?

You can see the resurrection difference for yourself beginning now. Come in deeper by faith than you have ever done before. Simply say, "Lord Jesus Christ, I need your forgiveness and invite you into my heart." Then go back into the world a new person, for that is what the Bible promises.

Linger in the uncertainty of halfheartedness no longer. Some of the unhappiest people in the church spend their lives in the semidarkness of shallow commitment. In D. L. Moody's words, "They have just enough religion to be miserable. They cannot be happy at a wild party and they are not happy at the church." Do not spend your life in predawn dubiety about who Jesus is and what he can do. Come to him completely as you take the elements of his Table.

A man, asked to serve on a church board, tried to dodge his responsibility. He said to his pastor, "Let someone else do it; I don't want to be tied down." "Why not?" the pastor asked. Then he pressed the matter: "Jesus was not tied down for you, my friend. He was nailed down!" The proof of what Jesus paid is symbolized by the Communion elements. That pastor's point is easy to see: If he who calls us to serve went to such great lengths for us, how can we ever imagine responding to his invitation with half-hearted devotion?

This principle of commitment applies to other areas of life too: It has its place in your marriage, in your relationship with your children, and on your job. It applies in the work of Christ's church. Only when we give ourselves with enthusiasm, all the way, do we find fulfillment.

The principle of going all the way with Christ is never more important than at the Lord's Supper. This is no place for the halfhearted. If you still look back longingly at the old life, allow the bread and cup of the Lord's Supper to pass you by. If, on the other hand, you have been to Calvary and have seen the empty tomb through the eyes of faith, you will want to partake at the Table for Christ's sake. Come with eyes and heart wide open to the possibility that he will do a new work in you today.

Oh, say! Can you see by the dawn's early light? Can you see in your own life the difference that Christ alone is making? If you cannot see, then there is no better morning than Easter and no better place than this Table to come to Jesus completely. When you do, you will see that he has loved you all the way through death, and that he loves you still!

Come, making the words of the old hymn your heart's desire:

> Open my eyes, that I may see
> Glimpses of truth Thou hast for me;
> Place in my hands the wonderful key
> That shall unclasp and set me free.
> Silently now I wait for Thee,
> Ready my God, Thy will to see;
> Open my eyes, illumine me, Spirit divine.

An Ulster-Scot, Robert Leslie Holmes is the minister of the First Presbyterian Church of Pittsburgh, Pennsylvania. His previous pastorates were in California, Florida, Georgia, and Mississippi. He earned his B.A. degree at the University of Mobile (Alabama), his M.Div. at Reformed Theological Seminary, and his doctorate at Columbia Theological Seminary. Through the media ministry of First Presbyterian Church, he is heard across the United States weekly. He has written previously for a variety of journals and magazines. He is the author of *Don't Try to Stop on a Mountaintop* (Fortson, Ga.: Fortson Press, 1997).

10

Come and Have Breakfast

WILLIAM H. HINSON

Just after daybreak, Jesus stood on the beach; but the disciples did not know that it was Jesus. Jesus said to them, "Children, you have no fish, have you?" They answered him, "No." He said to them, "Cast the net to the right side of the boat, and you will find some." So they cast it, and now they were not able to haul it in because there were so many fish. That disciple whom Jesus loved said to Peter, "It is the Lord!" When Simon Peter heard that it was the Lord, he put on some clothes, for he was naked, and jumped into the sea. But the other disciples came in the boat, dragging the net full of fish, for they were not far from the land, only about a hundred yards off. When they had gone ashore, they saw a charcoal fire there, with fish on it, and bread. Jesus said to them, "Bring some of the fish that you have just caught." So Simon Peter went aboard and hauled the net ashore, full of large fish, a hundred fifty-three of them; and though there were so many, the net was not torn. Jesus said to them, "Come and have breakfast."

John 21:4–12 NRSV

69

*J*ave you ever wondered how the fishermen of Galilee stayed in business? Every time Jesus asked them if they were catching anything, their answer was always no. Here they fished all night without catching a thing when the risen Christ, standing on the beach, inquired about their catch. When they admitted that their net was empty, he instructed them to cast on the right side of the boat. It was only after they made their cast and were unable to haul in the net because of the great quantity of fish that the disciples realized that their fishing director on the beach was the risen Lord. It was then that Jesus said, "Come and have breakfast." This was no ordinary meal to which they were invited. Ruptured relationships were about to be restored.

Repairing Ruptured Relationships

In the ancient Eastern world there were three common covenantal ways of cementing a once broken relationship. One was called the salt covenant. Salt was very precious. Our word *salary* comes from the word *salt.* So we speak of someone being "worth his or her salt." When President Reagan and Anwar Saddat reached a Middle East accord, they shared some salt.

Another ancient means of cementing a covenant in that part of the world might remind you of your wedding day: When two neighbors once at odds resolved their differences, they might publicly celebrate the restoration of their relationship by carrying one another over their tent or house threshold. This was known as the threshold covenant.

The most common way of celebrating a repaired relationship, however, was the meal covenant. Scripture contains many examples of persons reestablishing a relationship through a shared meal. In Genesis 14, Abraham and the kings of Salem and Sodom made a meal covenant, as did Laban and Jacob in Genesis 31.

Luke 15 brings another example of the meal covenant before us. After the father welcomed his prodigal son home with a ring, a robe, and shoes, he ordered the fatted calf killed and sat down to share a meal with his once estranged son. It was a relationship once ruptured but now restored. The elder brother, on the other hand, would not eat with someone he had not forgiven.

The best example of the meal covenant for us, however, is the Supper that was instituted by our Lord. It signifies our reconciliation to God through Christ's death on the cross.

The human family shares a universal need for reconciliation. Once I visited the Country Music Hall of Fame in Nashville, Tennessee. A large number of famous records were mounted on the walls and ceilings of the various rooms. Among them was "Won't Somebody Play Another Somebody Done Somebody Wrong Song?" We can resonate with the lyrics of that song. We have either had somebody do us wrong, or we have done somebody else wrong.

Reul Howe, the noted therapist, told a story of a little girl who, after having a fit of anger, was sent upstairs by her mother. A short time later the mother went upstairs and discovered that her angry child had taken a pair of scissors and cut up the mother's favorite dress. Crushed, the mother fell across the bed weeping. After a few moments the little girl began to tug at her mother's dress. Her mother turned and asked, "What do you want from me now?" The little girl responded, "Will you take me back?"

That is the cry of the whole human family. Like the little girl in the story we all need to be taken back at some time, and never more so than in our relationship with God. The good news of the gospel is that he always takes us back when we ask him. When we fail him, as the disciples did in the shadow of his cross, the response of our Lord is always the same: "Come and have breakfast." Jesus Christ wants to restore us—to reconcile us to God and have us reconciled to one another. That is incredibly good news!

Facing Up to Our Sins

Since Jesus wants to reconcile us, what can we do to help that happen? First of all, we must face some things about ourselves. Jesus always insists upon a self-examination. When Peter came running up to Jesus on the beach that morning, he surely noticed two things: first, that the caller on the shore was the risen Lord;

and second, that breakfast was being cooked on a charcoal fire. Peter remembered another fire, a fire in Caiaphas the High Priest's courtyard. Simon Peter would never forget that charcoal fire where he warmed his hands as he denied the Lord three times. Yet now it is not a fire of threat but a fire of invitation, for Christ never reminds us of our failures in order to hurt us but to heal us. "Come and have breakfast," he says.

Our Lord is strangely insistent in his positive desire for us to face our specific sins. He knows that after honestly facing some things about ourselves, we always realize that his forgiveness is necessary and always available. Moreover, as surely as we are forgiven persons, we must also be forgiving persons.

Jesus made it plain in the Lord's Prayer that we may expect our trespasses to be forgiven "as we forgive those who trespass against us." Do we realize what we are saying when we pray that prayer? We are saying we are willing to be forgiven in direct proportion to our willingness to forgive. That is a pretty big step for many of us.

Becoming Channels of Grace

Having faced some things about ourselves and having recognized that we must be forgiving persons in order to experience forgiveness, we must also conclude that only the Holy Spirit of God can provide us with the grace and strength to forgive those who have sinned against us. Forgiveness of the kind I am describing here is not a human possibility, but in Christ's strength we become channels of his grace.

Several months ago, a young woman shared her testimony in our church. She told a hushed congregation about being abducted by two men when she was only nineteen years old. She had arrived home from night classes at a local university and was about to enter her apartment when they assaulted her. One of the men shot her with a sawed-off shotgun just before daylight and left her beside the sidewalk to bleed to death. For a time the young woman, seeing all the blood she was losing, was desperately afraid that she would die right there on the sidewalk. Still conscious, her mind was filled with thoughts of her own death.

Thankfully, within minutes a passerby found her and called 911, and she was able to get the medical treatment she needed.

At the hospital the young woman began to reflect on what had happened to her. Suddenly she became afraid that she might not die. The agony of the attack was too much for her. That moment marked the beginning of a time in her life when she really wanted to commit suicide. A good therapist helped her to move beyond that stage, but he was unable to heal her of the bitterness and emptiness she felt. Finally, the young woman explained how she had turned, in desperation, to the church. The Sunday she chose to attend was Communion Sunday. She listened to a sermon on forgiveness and took the elements of Holy Communion. When she did, the love of Jesus filled her so miraculously that, for the first time in years, she was able to release her bitterness and anger. The love she experienced at the Lord's Table was so overwhelming that it not only healed her, but it also led her to write the two men who are now in prison. In that letter she offered them not only the Lord's forgiveness but her forgiveness as well. Today that radiant young woman is one of the leaders in our prison ministry. Her life demonstrates the good news of God's forgiving grace.

As we were preparing to move from Douglas, Georgia, to Savannah, Georgia, a distance of about 150 miles, a layman in our Douglas church brought a good-bye gift for our then two-year-old son, John. It was a kitten that was wild and untrained. The cat's behavior was so bad I had to transport him to Savannah in a lard can. Gus was not only wild and uncontrollable, he was the ugliest cat in Georgia. My wife and the children rode to Savannah on that hot summer day in the comfort of my mother-in-law's new car. I drove alone in a Volkswagen Beetle with no air-conditioning and a kitten in a lard can.

That cat yowled all the way to Savannah! The reverberating screams coming from the lard can gave me an Excedrin headache! My friendship with Gus got off to a rocky start. That, however, was only the beginning of a long and costly relationship. That cat carried with him a whole set of demands. Our son's cat would not eat any food except the expensive variety. He would not drink water out of a bowl or a saucer the way other cats do. He insisted on drinking in the bathtub with the water trickling down from the faucet into his mouth and throat. If the faucet trickle was too fast, the cat refused to drink and yowled some more. If it was too slow, he would yowl again. He was the most demanding cat I have ever known. My brothers, knowing I love dogs, frequently teased me about putting up with that cat.

Despite his obnoxious behavior, Gus the cat spent many years at the Hinson home. His final illness occurred when I was out of state at General Conference. His kidneys failed. Death was inevitable. My family insisted that the veterinarian keep the cat comfortable until I got back home, and he did through intravenous feeding and drugs. They wanted me to be present for Gus's funeral. The vet's bill for keeping the cat alive was so high he sent me a sympathy card along with the invoice.

Why did I, a dog lover, spend all that money on a fussy cat? It was because I learned to love him. I loved that cat, not because of how he behaved, but because he belonged to our son, John. During all of those childhood years when our son went to bed, whether happy or unhappy, Gus was always with him. I can still see John carrying Gus like a piece of stove wood, his legs hanging over John's arms and Gus's stomach sagging in between. My wife and I witnessed that ritual every night as our young son staggered up the stairs carrying that oversized cat. When we went up to say prayers with John, he and Gus would be sharing a pillow. Gus was always there for John. The relationship once ruptured in a hot VW Beetle was restored because of John's love for that cat.

That is essentially what the apostle Paul shouted throughout the Mediterranean world: "You belong to Christ!" Because we are all bound up with Jesus, God wants to share his amazing, transforming love with us. How can he love us so? We belong to Christ, that is why. A terrible price was paid for us. Our sins cost the life of God's Son. Through his cross, a ruptured relationship is restored.

The Lord's Table in our church sanctuary reminds us of the risen Lord who issues an incredible invitation: "Come and have breakfast with me." We can never be flippant about that forgiveness or assume that it is cheap. The cross on the Table stands there to remind us how much our forgiveness cost. God loves

74

and forgives us because we belong to Christ. "Come and have breakfast!"

The pastor of the largest United Methodist Church in the world, First Methodist Church of Houston, Texas, William H. Hinson is the author of several books, including *Solid Living in a Shattered World* (Nashville: Abingdon, 1983) and *Triumphant Living for Turbulent Times* (Wheaton: Victor, 1993). His most recent book is *Faith, Lies, and the Opinion Polls* (Wheaton: Victor, 1993). A Georgian, Dr. Hinson was educated at Georgia Southern University, Boston University, and earned his doctorate in theology at Candler School of Theology at Emory University.

11

The Feast
and the Future

NIGEL M. DE S. CAMERON

Truly I tell you, I will never again drink of the fruit
of the vine until that day when I drink it new in the
kingdom of God.

Mark 14:25 NRSV

*I*t is common for us to link advent and advent—the Christmas coming and the coming in the clouds—though we do
so less than we did when "Lo! He Comes with Clouds
Descending!" was a staple of the Sunday diet that prepared for
Christmas. We can hardly doubt the theological grounding of
this twin-track adventual dogma or its practical benefit in drawing our attention beyond the manger, beyond the cross, beyond
even the empty tomb, to ascension and even to the return, planting in the most popular of Christian feasts and the most acces-
sible of its doctrines a lasting memorial of what has proved the
most forgettable Christian belief that this same Jesus who
ascended will come again.

The Lord's Supper and Ascension

Not only will Christ come again, we will see him when he comes. In the meantime, through the eyes of our hearts, we see him at this Table. The Lord, before he ascended, designed his Supper to be both a celebration of his atoning death and an earnest sign of continuing presence while we await the coming kingdom. That, surely, was of central significance in his thinking about this Feast with so many names. Its pivotal position in the God-given liturgy of the church of God can never be understood as somehow placing ritual above the teaching of God's Word, or the fervent, doctrine-fed worship of his believing people. Here we have ritual firmly placed at the heart of the gospel: "I will never again drink of the fruit of the vine until that day when I drink it new in the kingdom of God." Whenever we do this, we at the same time proclaim the Lord's death and anticipate his kingdom.

God has planted at the heart of the life of the church the Feast of the New Passover, to be eaten in his absence as we wait in expectation: diligent servants eagerly at work, wise virgins with lamps trimmed, a people ready for the double summons to the glory and the righteousness of God, as salvation and damnation are brought to their final focus in the beginning of the end.

So is it not strange that this keystone message of the cornerstone Feast of the church has found its way to the very periphery of our evangelical vision? It is not just that evangelical faith in the doctrines of the life to come has been discounted. What of evangelical preaching? We need to ask not whether believers check the heaven and hell boxes when they are asked but how much it matters to them to find them on the survey form at all.

In addition, we must ask why their pastors and teachers evade the primary message of the New Testament concerning the future Jesus: He went to heaven with a promise to come again and set up a kingdom that shall have no end. In the meantime, he asks his church to remember him. We have yet to plumb the depth of this withdrawal from a central confidence in our personal and common future, which down through faithful centuries has been the very pivot of the believer's confidence and the bastion of piety.

The exemplary character of Holy Scripture suggests a model for our preaching and teaching that has fallen from fashion just as the degrading of the life of the body of Christ has reached new depths.

The Supper Proclaims the Lord's Death

This small statement takes us to the heart of the cross of Jesus Christ and its memorializing in the Supper, for it raises the question of the relevancy of what happened then to what happens now. It is interesting to note that this is an issue even in that first generation of the apostolic church. The passage of time has begun to be noted, and with its extension, the relation of the first coming and the second begins to take on sharper significance and raises questions for devotion and for theology. The Lord's death is past; it is to be proclaimed—and indeed, that proclamation is the very rationale for the church. The missionary logic of the gospel—not just Judea and Samaria but the uttermost parts of the earth—is glimpsed in undying tension with its confidence in the blessed hope. This same Jesus will return, but first the gospel must be preached to all nations.

In addition, the Feast of the Cross with its earnest looking forward to the messianic banquet finds itself enrolled as proclamation. The Feast of the Lord's Death is the badge of the church's testimony in the world. This cross-feast is given to shape the life of the believing community that we might feed on the Living Bread of God now gone to sit at the right hand of the Father. This is so that, in the meantime, we would be nourished both for our souls and for the testimony of our cruciform church and selves.

In the ritual of the Feast we are connected by an indelible succession of apostolic proclamations with the first Feast, the Supper itself at which our Lord washed feet and broke bread and poured wine; at which he lay back on the breast of his beloved disciple: as the Passover he had desired to eat and for which he had made such particular arrangements gave place to the anticipatory celebration of the dying of another lamb, this one slain not in Moses' day but from the very foundation of the world—whose body will yet bear those dear tokens of his passion to all eternity as manhood taken into Godhead remains gloriously scarred to all ages.

The Supper Proclaims the Kingdom to Come

"Truly I tell you, I will never again drink of the fruit of the vine until that day when I drink it new in the kingdom of God." The kingdom, let us remember, has its sense of being and of not yet being, the now and the not yet. Our memorializing of his saving passion must be projected through resurrection, ascension, and second coming to the kingdom that shall have no end. It is, therefore, a meal of the past, the present, and the future.

The Supper is as much a meal of the future as of the present and the past. It is as much anticipated as devotion and recollection. Such is the subject who is recalled and to whom is devotion that we remember his departure, and his early return becomes the pulsating hope of the Table fellowship. The very public character of the hoped-for kingdom takes on its final and lasting eternal significance as the end of history. Creation and redemption come together. The uncreated Word, through whom all things were made, took the form of a servant. He was obedient to death, even death on a cross. He will be highly exalted and will lead captivity captive. He will then take his place at the right hand of the Majesty on high. He has risen from that place to return glorious to the fight in the closing stage of history and the culmination of the eternal purposes of God. This is the final chapter in the story of his triumph through the cross: "You will see the Son of Man seated at the right hand of the Power, and 'coming with the clouds of heaven'" (Mark 14:62).

So the proclamation of the cross and its Supper is, finally, the sacrament of the wedding feast, the Supper of the bridegroom and his bride. Every time we eat the bread and drink from the cup, we remember he has gone from us in a physical sense but for only a while, and we sit awaiting that day when he will join us again.

Nigel M. de S. Cameron, a minister in the Church of Scotland, is an English-born Scotsman who holds degrees from Cambridge University and Edinburgh University, where he completed his Ph.D. studies in 1982. A prolific writer, he is currently Provost at Trinity International University in Deerfield, Illinois. The former chairman of the Center for Bioethics and Public Policy in London, England, he is a contributing editor to *Christianity Today.* Most recently he has served as a general editor of *Calvin's Old Testament Commentaries: The Rutherford House Translation* (Grand Rapids: Eerdmans, 1992).

12

Keeping the Feast with Our Lord

JOHN MCINTOSH

When the hour came, he took his place at the table, and the apostles with him. He said to them, "I have eagerly desired to eat this Passover with you before I suffer; for I tell you, I will not eat it until it is fulfilled in the kingdom of God." Then he took a cup, and after giving thanks he said, "Take this and divide it among yourselves; for I tell you that from now on I will not drink of the fruit of the vine until the kingdom of God comes." Then he took a loaf of bread, and when he had given thanks, he broke it and gave it to them, saying, "This is my body, which is given for you. Do this in remembrance of me." And he did the same with the cup after supper, saying, "This cup that is poured out for you is the new covenant in my blood."

Luke 22:14–20 NRSV

What do you expect when you celebrate the Lord's Supper? Assurance of faith and joy in God are what our Lord intended for you. The more's the pity then that Christians disagree about its meaning!

Holy Communion is another word we use, from 1 Corinthians 10:16. There you and I are reminded that to eat the bread and drink of the cup when we remember Christ is to share together in the benefits and significance of his death.

Eucharist, which means *thanksgiving*, may sound strange to you if you are in the Protestant tradition. Yet that name faithfully reflects the atmosphere of the celebration Jesus held with his disciples on the night he was betrayed. There was much thanksgiving and praise to God for his power and redeeming grace. Why?

God's deliverance of Israel from the bondage of Egypt in the exodus was his great act of salvation in the Old Testament. The Jews were right to celebrate its memory in the Feast of the Passover with deep and joyful gratitude.

Moreover, as a Christian, you know how our Lord's "exodus" or departure in his death and resurrection assures you and me of God's smile and forgiveness and blessing forever in the world to come!

That's why the Lord commanded us all to remember him by celebrating the fact of his willing death on the cross as a sacrifice "for the sins of many." He wanted us never to forget that that was the central thing he came to do. It was the climactic moment of his whole earthly ministry.

To celebrate the Supper in remembrance of him is Christ's own remedy for those moments when we forget God's love for us. This is Christ's way of reminding us that we belong together. You are heirs with Christ of the restored and perfected creation. Not even Adam and Eve in the Garden had such joyful communion with the Lord God as you and I will enjoy together as permanent guests of Christ's table in the kingdom to come.

Look with me at what the Holy Spirit inspired Luke to record for us about how Jesus commanded us to remember him. He did this as he himself joined his disciples to celebrate the Passover. Imagine yourself as one of Christ's chosen in the Upper Room.

At the Feast of the Passover

As a Jew, you are there with the Lord both to remember your deliverance from Egypt many centuries ago, but still very present to you, and to rejoice in your hope, your expectation of a second deliverance under the Messiah from the power of Rome. Earlier this Thursday afternoon your Passover lamb was slaughtered in the temple and its blood splashed on the altar. It is evening and, by Jewish reckoning, the early part of Friday. You and the other disciples are reclining, not sitting, with your left elbow on the table supporting your head.

You know what usually happens. First, there is a preliminary first cup of wine, always in those days diluted about 50 percent with water. As the "father" presiding for the Passover group gives thanks, he always calls this first cup "the fruit of the vine." Next, he takes a mixture of "bitter herbs," dips them in salt water, and gives them to all of you.

After that, a second cup of wine is poured but not drunk until, in a family situation, a son of the father asks why this feast. The father then reminds all present of the story of God's promises to your father Abraham. He recalls their fulfillment in the exodus and the giving of the Law at Mount Sinai. Together you sing Psalms 113 and 114 to express your praise and thanksgiving to God for his mighty acts of redeeming mercy and power. Now you drink the second cup.

Then comes the main part of the meal: The father explains that the bitter herbs are the bitterness of Israel's affliction in Egypt; the unleavened bread on the table is the haste in which they had to leave their affliction—no time to bake bread with yeast in it—and it is called "the bread of affliction." The Passover lamb represents God's "passing over" and sparing the households where the blood of the lamb was sprinkled on door frames.

You begin eating when the person presiding takes one of the two large cakes of unleavened bread on the table and breaks it into pieces. This symbolizes your poverty in Egypt for there you had only pieces, not whole loaves. He gives thanks. You break off a couple of pieces, put bitter herbs between them, and dip this into a puree of dates and raisins and vinegar. About this time, you notice Judas slipping away sneakily. You eat your portion of the second unleavened bread cake with bitter herbs and follow that with a piece of the Passover lamb itself.

After that, you see the third cup poured, and grace after meat is said. This third cup is particularly important; it is the cup of blessing. A special thanksgiving to God is spoken over it. Perhaps you remembered with great gladness at this point how in the desert, after God's covenant of the Ten Commandments and other ordinances were ratified by the blood of bulls, Moses and the seventy elders could ascend the mountain and, in the visible presence of God, celebrate the anticipated blessing by eating and drinking.

Finally, you sing Psalms 115 through 118 over a fourth and final cup. Your heart is filled with praise to the Lord for his lovingkindness and faithfulness to Israel. You drink the fourth cup. The feast is over. In the company of fellow disciples, you have enjoyed several hours of solemn, yet joyful and spontaneous, celebration of God's redeeming love. This night, however, is different.

Jesus Makes It Different

Almost from the beginning, you notice Jesus has his own way of doing things. First, there is his intense and eager anticipation of joining with you in a final special act before his imminent suffering.

Second, you see that he is also looking far beyond your present hope of some earthly restoration of Israel. Only half-comprehendingly you hear him say this will be his last Passover until it is fulfilled; that is, until all that it ever pointed to has become a reality in the kingdom of God. This will be God's perfect reign over his restored creation. It is something far better than the Garden of Eden, better than the Promised Land, or even the restoration of Israel that Jesus came to bring about; better because the kingdom of God will be the final and perfected goal, which that first sinless state, and Israel at its greatest, only foreshadowed. Just as the original Passover was preliminary to Israel's entry into the land flowing with milk and honey, so Jesus looks forward at this Passover to the joy of the new creation and wants you and me to do the same.

What is really different, though, is that Jesus makes the meal point toward heaven. But, how does a meal point to heaven? Because even an ordinary meal of family or friends celebrating some occasion is something you keenly anticipate. So much the more a gathering in which you joy in your common blessings in

God. You know, as Jesus does, that the presence of God with his people is frequently seen in Scripture as a cause for fullness of joy and life, just as expulsion from the Garden and thus from God's presence was itself immediate death.

As you hear Jesus' words about eating the Passover in the kingdom of God, you instantly recall the supreme picture of joy in God's presence and blessing in Scripture—that of being a guest at his Table. You are reminded of Isaiah's description of a coming "feast of rich food, a feast of well-aged wines" on the mountain, where Jerusalem lies, the city of God's presence (25:6–8). Perhaps later you will remember Jesus' own frequent depiction of the kingdom of God as a feast or a wedding banquet. These are the first two differences you notice.

The third difference is that as Jesus gives thanks for the first cup, traditionally given the name "the fruit of the vine," and hands it to you and the others, you hear him say that he will not drink it "until the kingdom of God comes." You cannot help but notice his emphasis on God's coming reign of blessing. At the same time, you begin to understand that he is really going to be leaving you until that time.

Clearly this is no ordinary Passover Jesus presides over! What will he change next? You arrive now at the main part of the meal: The roasted Passover lamb and the large cake of unleavened bread are on the table, waiting to be broken and shared around. Here Jesus makes a startling fourth change by renaming "the bread of affliction" as "my body given for you."

You are stunned. No longer will you think of the hurried escape from affliction of your fathers. From now on, as you eat this bread, you will think of the unthinkable: Jesus your Lord is your Passover Lamb. He is offering himself as a sacrifice so that you might escape just death for your sin and guilt.

Perhaps the meal goes on in silence now as you and the other disciples still find it too hard to take in Jesus' words about his coming suffering and bodily self-sacrifice. A solemn note is mixed with the usual joy and expectation as you drink the second cup.

But Jesus has yet one more equally amazing change to introduce: The main part of the Passover meal is now over, but your traditional celebration of God's great deliverance of his people is not quite finished. You are about to drink the climactic "cup of blessing" when Jesus reinterprets even this: No longer are you to do this in remembrance of Moses and the old covenant of law; henceforth you will think instead of Jesus' blood about to be shed in sacrifice for you. He calls it the new covenant of the forgiveness of your sins.

You drink from the cup Jesus blesses God for; mindful as you do that the words of the prophet Jeremiah about the new covenant of forgiveness are in Christ's mind, as are also the prophet Isaiah's words about God's suffering servant, pouring "out himself to death" to bear "the sin of many" (Isaiah 53:12).

Only after Jesus' death on the cross, his resurrection from the dead, and the coming of the Holy Spirit does all this make sense for you. Only after Pentecost do you realize how it is that Jesus can speak of coming joy in feasting with God with you and me at the very moment he contemplates his coming, horrific suffering. His finished work of sacrificial death in your place opens the kingdom of heaven to all believers.

So the "Lord's Supper," as the Holy Spirit inspired the apostle Paul to call Jesus' interpretation of the fulfilled meaning of the Passover supper, is vitally important for you and will be forevermore. It focuses your heart and mind where Jesus wants it focused: on the central reality of his death for your forgiveness. He wants your confidence in him and your love of him to grow day by day. Along with that, your hope, your eager expectation, like his, of perfect joy at God's table in his coming kingdom.

John McIntosh, an Australian Anglican minister, is Associate Professor of Missions at Reformed Theological Seminary in Jackson, Mississippi. Previously he served as a pastor in Australia and a missionary to the Batak people of Indonesia. He was on the faculty of the University of Nommensen, Indonesia, and served as Principal of the Federal Training College of the Church Missionary Society in Sydney, Australia. He earned a B.A. at the University of Sydney, a B.D. and M.Th. at Westminster Theological Seminary, and a Doctor of Missiology from Trinity Evangelical Divinity School.

13

Life from the Lord

WILLIAM C. BROWNSON

Jesus said to them, "Very truly, I tell you, unless you eat the flesh of the Son of Man and drink his blood, you have no life in you. Those who eat my flesh and drink my blood have eternal life, and I will raise them up on the last day; for my flesh is true food and my blood is true drink. Those who eat my flesh and drink my blood abide in me, and I in them."

John 6:53–56 NRSV

*T*wo men, one a friend of mine, stood outside a lavish country estate. They had come to make repairs on some of the buildings. They looked about them in amazement. Here was a huge colonial mansion with three gleaming, late-model cars in its garage. Nearby were tennis courts, a swimming pool, a stable for horses; and all around rolled acres of lush green lawn. One of the workers shook his head and sighed, "Man, that's the life!" "No," my friend, Ray, responded, "Jesus Christ is the life." Which one do you think had it right? What is the life?

Both were speaking, of course, of something more than bare survival. They were talking about "quality of life"—a kind of living that yields joy and fulfillment. Both had in mind what all of us deeply feel: There is more to human life than a beating heart.

We call people "alive" or "dead" in a number of ways, do we not? We describe a sound sleeper, for example, as "dead to the world." He is alive, but he does not respond to what is happening around him. Bright lights, music, persistent prodding—all fail to rouse him. He seems, at least for the time, gone from the realm of sense experience.

Once I visited a long ward at Mercy Hospital in Chicago. Across the aisle from my friend lay a man who had been struck on the head by a swinging steel beam. He had been in this ward, I learned, for many weeks. He was breathing; he seemed awake; his eyes were fixed in a vacant stare. No glimmer of consciousness, no light of recognition, would ever again brighten his face. He was dead to the world of the mind.

Warm and breathing, yet not really alive. Could that be said also of some who are physically alert and mentally keen? Can personalities that seem vibrant and vital yet remain, at some deeper level, lifeless? Can human beings be "dead to the world of the spirit," unresponsive to the things of God? Apparently so. Jesus said as much in one of his most startling pronouncements. Listen: "Very truly, I tell you, unless you eat the flesh of the Son of Man and drink his blood, you have no life in you" (John 6:53).

The Walking Dead

What can he mean by that? We know who the Son of Man is. That is Jesus' favorite term for himself, his code name. But, what is this about "eating his flesh" and "drinking his blood"? Does he really intend to say that apart from him we have no life whatsoever? Yes; in his eyes, we are the walking dead.

In the Bible's thought world, God is the source and giver of life: physical vitality, mental acumen, and also the life that is life indeed. This deeper kind can be known only by God's human creatures. Only of humankind was it said God "breathed into his nostrils the breath of life; and the man became a living being" (Genesis 2:7). We alone are made in God's likeness for a special

relationship with him. This is our humanness. We are made for
God, for covenant relationship with him. In that fellowship with
the Life-giver, we find our true life.

However, when the bond of harmony between Creator and
creature is broken, life ebbs away. In disobedience, we have shattered that bond. We chose to go our own way, to declare our
independence. In such a context we found God's word of warning accurate: "You shall not eat of the fruit . . . or you shall die"
(Genesis 3:3).

Not that we experience physical death the moment we disobey. That rarely happens, if at all. However, something within
us dies. We are like branches newly broken from a tree. Our
leaves still appear green and supple, our branches healthy and
firm, but the forces of death have begun their work in us. Away
from God, we are like cut flowers. We keep our borrowed beauty
for the moment but soon wither and fade. We have lost touch
with our source of life.

Life through His Death

Jesus promises that we can find life again in him. That is the
significance of all the "life-words" he compared himself variously
as, Bread of Life, Light of Life, Water of Life, Life eternal. He
came here, said he, that we might have life, and have it abun-
dantly (compare John 10:10).

Still, there is more to Jesus' claim. He tells his hearers that all
their hopes of life are tied up with his "flesh and blood." "Unless
you eat the flesh of the Son of Man, and drink his blood, you have
no life in you." Think about that expression. It obviously means
the blood separated from the flesh. That suggests not life but death.

Remember Shylock in Shakespeare's *The Merchant of Venice*?
He was the creditor who demanded a grisly sort of payment if
his debtor defaulted: a pound of flesh. When the time limit
expired, things looked bad for the man in debt. However, the
clever "judge" in this case foiled Shylock. He ruled that Shylock could take his pound of flesh, but if in so doing he shed
blood, he would lose his own life.

The judge was demanding the impossible. Flesh and blood cling together in all of us. When they are torn asunder, we begin to die. That, ultimately, is the thought beneath the surface in Jesus' words. He points to the death he will soon experience. It will be a kind of self-offering for others, a sacrifice for the sins of the world. He says our hope will depend on his dying. We will find life through his death.

Some find this hard to accept. "Do you mean that we are dependent for real life not only on this person, Jesus, but on his dying a terrible death?" In our Lord's time, such teaching offended many people. For Jews, anyone who died on a cross was considered accursed. How could this horrible event help anyone?

Even the disciples could not comprehend it at first. When Jesus began to speak of his approaching death, Peter protested. "God forbid it, Lord! This must never happen to you" (Matthew 16:22). The idea that the King of Israel, the Hope of the nations, the Savior of the world, should have to die in rejection and shame seemed unthinkable.

In truth, however, we touch here an even deeper offense. The death of Jesus underlines the extent of our need, the depth of our sin. How urgent and deadly the human problem must be if it takes this tragedy to deal with it! "Surely our situation isn't that bad!" we protest. Regardless of that, the Bible's witness is unwavering. In a world like ours, a world of rampant hatred, of violence and death, there is no remedy for human sin except in a cross. There God takes upon his own breaking heart the worst that evil can do. Christ must be given up to death. His body must be broken. His blood must be poured out. Then, strangely, like a lily from a putrid marsh, life springs up from the Savior's death.

Partaking of Christ

I find one more startling element in these words of Jesus about life. Listen again: "Very truly, I tell you, unless you eat the flesh of the Son of Man and drink his blood, you have no life in you." Life comes only from Jesus, only by his death, and only to those who *partake* of his flesh and blood. What can that mean? The thought of it must have been abhorrent to Jewish hearers. Jewish law expressly forbids drinking blood.

"Eating" and "drinking" in this context, however, are action pictures of what it means to believe. For one thing, they are voluntary, personal acts. The hunger strikes of prisoners and martyrs are proof of that. No one is compelled to eat. You can keep a man alive for a while by intravenous feeding, but no power on earth can make him chew and swallow if he refuses to. He must so *choose*. Believing in Christ calls for personal decision also. Parents, friends, ministers, teachers cannot do it for us.

The image conveys even more. What we eat and drink becomes, in a literal sense, part of us. You've heard it dozens of times: "We are what we eat." Portions of our meals are assimilated into the living tissue of our bodies. Partaking of food thus points to the most profound reality in our faith: receiving Christ. When we trust in Jesus, accepting him as our Savior and Lord, he enters our lives by his Spirit and imparts to us his own life. Jesus put it this way: "Those who eat my flesh and drink my blood abide in me, and I in them" (John 6:56). Faith brings about a vital union between believers and their Lord. Jesus himself, enthroned in our hearts, becomes our life.

The Lord's Supper is a rich reminder and confirming seal of this new life in Christ. There the "eating" and "drinking" of faith find beautiful expression. Receiving the bread and partaking of the cup in faith brings to us assurance that his body was broken for us and that his blood was poured out on our behalf. What is more, he is forever our nourishment and strength. At his Table we not only remember him and anticipate his return, we experience with him a sharing of life. How then can people like us "come alive"? How can we stop merely existing and begin to live in the Lord's way? We begin by realizing our need of him. We acknowledge he died for us and welcome him by faith as our Savior and Lord. By the Spirit's power, we are "born again."

There is more to come: Jesus called it life "more abundant." All that vitalizes our relationships, renews our zest for living, and makes us new, whole, happy persons, roots in a growing faith, a deepening fellowship with the Lord of life. We become more and more "rooted and grounded" in him, more and more a people fully alive.

My question to you is: Have you found the life he offers? Are you ready to receive him, the crucified and risen One? Many good things around us (like those my friend saw at the country estate) may enhance our "standard of living," but they can never impart life. They cannot make us "come alive." For that we need a life given for us and a life-giver. We need Jesus.

William C. Brownson, Reformed Church in America, is President Emeritus of *Words of HOPE.* He was born in Charlotte, North Carolina, and earned his A.B. degree at Davidson College there. After graduating from Columbia Theological Seminary in Decatur, Georgia, he earned his Th.D. in New Testament studies from Princeton Theological Seminary. He served as Professor of Preaching at Western Theological Seminary after serving Reformed churches in New Jersey and Illinois. Formerly president of the Reformed Church in America, Dr. Brownson has had a widespread radio ministry. He is the author of seventeen books, including *Courage to Pray* (Grand Rapids: Baker, 1989) and *Meeting Jesus* (Grand Rapids: Baker, 1993).

14

Communion: Healing for the Body

DERL G. KEEFER

The one who betrays me is with me, and his hand is on the table.

Luke 22:21 NRSV

*M*aking my way across the parking lot to my church, I noticed that someone had dropped a glass bottle. Particles were scattered all along the pavement. Those broken pieces of glass reminded me of God's church. The church too is splintered into theological camps and denominational lines, harassed by personality egos, damaged by gossip, betrayed, and attacked by Satanic forces. How the body needs healing! Only Christ can accomplish this miracle.

Greek linguists used an adjective to describe time. They said that time wiped out all things, as if a mind were a chalkboard and time an eraser, which wiped it clean. There are, however, some things time has not changed.

As Jesus sat in the Upper Room with his disciples almost two thousand years ago, he was aware of how easily the mind forgets. After all, his betrayer sat with him at the table, signifying not only that Judas had forgotten how far Christ had brought him and who Jesus was but the force that brings division in the church then and now. In that context, Jesus chose two ordinary objects to facilitate the disciples' memory of him and his objective in coming to earth. Bread and juice would become symbols of his body and blood. Every single time these disciples would participate in this ritual it would remind them of their faith. Christians throughout the ages would acquire a quickening of their faith as they participated in Holy Communion.

Bread was made through a process of beating the grains of wheat out by the heavy strokes of the flail then being ground into flour between heavy millstones. Finally, dough was made from the flour, formed into loaves, and baked in a hot oven. Christ told his followers that just as the bread had to be prepared in this way to be fit for use, so his body would be beaten and broken for their benefit. The breaking happened as he predicted it would when he was flogged in Caiaphas's palace and scourged in Pilate's hall. The mountain of the sin of the world weighed and pressed his spirit and mind in the agonizing moments on Calvary's hill as his body struggled in agony and pain.

The grape, the fruit of the vine, was placed under the press until the juice flowed out in a steady stream of purple liquid. Jesus said that in the same way his blood too would flow for the redemption of humankind. His prophecy came to fruition in Gethsemane's garden when he sweated great drops of blood. On the cross the butchers spread Christ's loving hands on the crossbars and pierced them through with great long spikes as the blood splattered. His head was crowned with thorns in an ugly portrayal of a ruling king's crown as blood flowed down his face and matted into his beard. In the end a spear pierced his side as blood gushed onto the ground, all for our salvation and purification.

At the foot of the cross, the church, collectively and individually, is healed of its sins. Because of this we rely on Communion to be holy, sacred, and precious. Only through ignorance is Communion ever considered mundane, routine, or dull. Communion reveals the healing power of God.

Healing Begins with an Invitation

Scholars note that Scripture in general, and the Gospels in particular, always take for granted that God is the great Initiator of life. Jehovah is the Alpha and Omega, the First and the Last, upon whom all else depends! In him all things find purpose and hold together.

God provided Communion for our benefit to strengthen our faith and to bind us together as one with each other and with the church that is already in heaven. Humankind did not invent this Holy Feast. The Father through his Son, Jesus, gives us an invitation to come and dine at the Table of faith with him! This invitation includes forgiveness from sin that has wedged man from God and from other people. This invitation also includes justification, the declaration of the acquittal of sinners from their past of sin. This invitation includes reconciliation, the restoration of relationships between man and God, and between people. There is once again a joy of fellowship between the created and the Creator.

After many lives were lost in the Alps due to defective ropes, the Alpine Club took up the matter to attempt to make the ropes safe and secure. After a long discussion of how to control the ropes that were to be sold, it was decided that the Alpine Club would inspect the composition of the materials in the ropes. To guarantee safety and quality, each rope would be marked by a crimson thread sown into them by the club members. Similarly, Jesus has sown a thread of relationship throughout all humankind to secure our safety.

Healing Gives Strength to an Aching Heart

The shattered glass I discovered along the parking lot typifies many lives. An aching heart results from death, addiction, abuse, accidents, gossip, infidelity, rape, age, harsh words, doubt, bigotry, bitterness, and much more. All these ravage the heart and bring crippling disease that no surgeon's scalpel can reach; but God offers healing now. If you need strength to withstand life's pressures, turn to God. He has many healing instruments to cure

95

hearts infected by hurt. His instruments of healing include love, caring friends, changing circumstances, new understanding, fresh beginnings, new outlooks, new friends, and a new lifestyle. He even promises to give us new hearts.

A general had won many victories. The king wanted to see the amazing sword used by the general to accomplish these victories on his campaigns. After careful examination of the weapon, the king returned the sword with a message: "Tell the general that I find his sword no better than any other." The general sent back his reply: "Tell the king that he should have sent also for the arm that is accustomed to wielding the sword."

In like fashion, God wields the sword of strength for us. Communion reminds us of his power to do so!

Healing Brings Fellowship

Imagine you were asked to find synonyms for the word *fellowship*. The synonyms you suggest will be included in a thesaurus soon to be published. What words would you write in your thesaurus? *Friendship, brotherhood, harmony, devotion, fraternity, corporate body, gang,* and *society* are some that might be included.

Some relationships are broken almost beyond repair. They are like the glass strewn on the parking lot of the church. Friendship, harmony, or a love bond may be shattered beyond recognition. Words, actions, insinuations, expressions, and attitudes can abort the fellowship of believers. Within the church body, this abortion of fellowship can be earth shattering. It can impede the church's numerical and spiritual growth, discourage new converts, lower morale, limit vision, ruin building programs, dampen corporate and individual worship, eliminate production, and reduce stewardship. If split fellowship has occurred within the family of God, it must be healed quickly. Each participant must be willing to work hard at harmonizing with each other and with God. Fellowship will be achieved if we sense God's love, acceptance, and forgiveness! Jesus modeled this for us.

A young woman was employed by an artist to sit as a model in his studio. She rummaged through some of his unfinished paintings one day while waiting for him to start on her portrait.

Noticing an unfinished picture of the crucifixion, she asked the painter who that wicked man on the cross was and what crime he had committed to be punished in such a manner.

The artist gave her a rather grudging answer to her questions. He coldly let her know he had no sympathy for the man on the cross and did not appreciate the Christian faith or lifestyle. Still, he acknowledged that some people believe he died for them. The young model responded, "I would think you would love him if he died for you." There are millions like the artist who do not love Jesus and who want no fellowship with him.

For Christians, Communion is a reminder of Christ's fellowship with us and our fellowship with him. It also reminds us of our need for fellowship with others in the human race.

Healing Ends with Celebration and Joy

Jesus came to earth with one specific goal: to die for a lost world. The end was nearing, and the stress, strain, and suffering as the human/divine sacrifice on the cross lay ahead. Before his disciples at the Passover Table, Jesus previewed the reason for his coming. He bared his concern with his followers there. Alongside the glumness appear two emotions seemingly foreign to the occasion—joy and celebration.

Interwoven in the conversation between Jesus and his followers are the assurance and confidence of the new kingdom of promise. Thanksgiving was offered through blessing and prayer. Every Passover includes praise and hope in psalm. Throughout the blackness of night, the light of spiritual victory pulsates in the words of Jesus. Communion celebrates the victory that Jesus won for everyone who participates in his sacrifice. As we gather at the Communion altar, it is to celebrate his victory over death, the grave, and hell. Every Communion is a confirmation of our acceptance by God through Christ, of our acceptance of Jesus into our lives, and of our acceptance of one another. The joy of the Lord is our strength.

Communion is the healing sacrament available to all who desire to know Jesus as Savior and Lord. The sacrament of the Lord's Supper is an expression of eternal and universal relevance to humankind. It is symbolic of God's personal desire for healing the whole world of sin. Through participation in Communion, each person is filled with dignity, purpose, and hope. Come, accept God's invitation to partake of the elements as brothers and sisters, with genuine humility and joyous faith.

Derl G. Keefer, a minister in the Church of the Nazarene, pastors a congregation in Three Rivers, Michigan. His previous pastorates were in Indiana and Illinois. He earned his B.A. degree at Southern Nazarene University and his Master's of Divinity at Nazarene Theological Seminary. Professional journals in which his sermons have appeared include *Preaching, Clergy Journal,* and *Resource Magazine,* as well as *Preachers' Manual* and *Clergy Journals Annual Manual.*

15

Lest We Forget

David C. Fisher

> The cup of blessing that we bless, is it not a sharing in the blood of Christ? The bread that we break, is it not a sharing in the body of Christ? Because there is one bread, we who are many are one body, for we all partake of the one bread. Consider the people of Israel; are not those who eat the sacrifices partners in the altar?
>
> 1 Corinthians 10:16–18 NRSV

Nothing is more characteristic of the Christian faith than this holy meal. That's been true from the very beginning. Our text illustrates the centrality of the Lord's Supper in the early church. In fact, Paul goes to great lengths to point out to the Corinthian church that this holy meal is grounded in an unbroken apostolic tradition.

A Sacramental Source

The Gospel stories are filled with instances of Jesus eating with people. There was something about Jesus and meals. His delight

99

in table fellowship with the most unlikely characters seems to be one of the signs of his kingdom.

The night before he died, he gathered his disciples together for a last supper. It was a Passover meal, a sacred meal for the people of Israel. Jesus transformed it into a holy meal for his new people, the church. The very next week, after his resurrection, Jesus stopped by to eat with people.

The early church continued the tradition. The Book of Acts, a history of the early church, is bracketed by the Lord's Supper. Acts 2 says one of the characteristics of the early church was breaking bread, shorthand for the Lord's Supper. At the end of Paul's ministry, he gathered the church at Ephesus to say good-bye (Acts 20), and they broke bread.

From the very beginning, it seems, God wrote something sacramental deep in the heart of his people. God gave the Passover, a sacred meal, to Israel; he gave the Lord's Supper to his church. At this holy meal, God binds us to Christ and binds us to each other. This meal binds us to history, the church through the ages, and it binds us to eternity.

In today's church we continue this unbroken tradition, now two thousand years old. We partake of something that packs the power of eternity at a table God designed to unify his people. It is, after all, a family meal.

Sacramental Strife

Yet, it must be said that this unifying sacrament has been an instrument of division. It is a tragic episode of Christian history. The Reformation of the church in the sixteenth century got off to a rousing start. In Germany, Martin Luther swayed the masses with his writings and persuaded German princes to join his cause. He was convinced that the gospel would sweep over the entire world. Germany awoke from medieval slumber.

At the same time, in Switzerland, Ulrich Zwingli believed the gospel and began his own Reformation. His reforming movement swept through the Swiss cantons like a flood. It was the Protestant Reformation.

100

Barely ten years into the Reformation, the reforming parties thought it wise to have the two old warriors meet to form an alliance. The delegations met for four days in Marburg, Germany. They drew up a 15-point statement of faith and principles. Luther and Zwingli agreed on 14.9 points.

The fifteenth point was about the Lord's Supper, and the two reformers agreed in principle. Both agreed that Christ is present at his Supper, but the nature of that presence divided them. Luther maintained Christ's presence was physical; Zwingli said it was spiritual.

The last day of the colloquy, the great reformers faced each other for the last time. Both were loaded for bear. As Zwingli came into the room, Luther was writing something in chalk on the table. He covered it with a silk cloth. The discussion began and Zwingli threw out a final challenge. He challenged Luther to find a single Scripture verse to support his position that Christ was physically present in the bread and wine of Communion.

Luther whipped the cloth off the table. There in bold print was his evidence: *Hoc est corpus meum* (that, by the way, is where the term *hocus-pocus* came from!). It is Latin for "This is my body"—Jesus' words at the Last Supper.

Zwingli rose to the occasion. The Renaissance man knew his languages. He replied to Luther that Jesus did not speak Latin! Zwingli reminded Luther that in Aramaic, the language Jesus spoke, there is no verb *is* in that sentence. Jesus must have meant the bread signified his body. After all, Jesus was in his earthly body when he declared this bread to be his body. If, then, the bread is his body, the incarnation is denied. Jesus cannot be incarnate and physically present in a million pieces of bread at the same time. Luther had an answer. He called on the medieval distinction between accidence and substance and named his doctrine The Ubiquity of Christ. It means Christ's physical body is in one place and everywhere at the same time.

Zwingli declared that was medieval nonsense. He had his own proof text, John 6:63, where Jesus says, "The spirit gives life; the flesh counts for nothing" (NIV). He told Luther, "The physical means nothing; it's spirit that counts. This text will break your neck."

Luther replied that German necks were thicker and harder to break than Swiss necks. The debate got hotter and, according to one report, Luther took a knife and carved *Hoc est corpus meum* into the table. The Marburg Colloquy ended in substantial agreement and in failure. The Reformation divided itself down the middle.

The tragedy was made larger by Zwingli's untimely death shortly after Marburg. His unlikely successor in the Swiss Reformation was a lawyer named John Calvin. Calvin was also a Renaissance humanist but a theologian too. He developed a mediating position between Zwingli's mere memorial and Luther's physical sacrament. Calvin was convinced that if he could get Luther in a room, they would agree. However, by that time the lines were too heavily drawn, and the two never met.

Now, after nearly five hundred years, a growing number of theologians, Lutheran, Reformed, and even some Catholic, believe and teach Calvin's view.

The Centrality of the Sacrament

Why retell this sad story? Well, beneath the story and running straight through our text and the following chapters are themes the old reformers and St. Paul teach. We need to know the story and the texts. After all, this sacrament is still part of the life of the church and we are here once again at the Table. What does it mean?

For one thing, all agree: The Lord's Table is central to the life of the church and its members. This sacrament is something believed and practiced in the church always, everywhere, and by all (the most general definition of orthodoxy). Paul goes to great pains to tell the Corinthian church that this Table is a non-negotiable fact of church life, something that is bedrock apostolic tradition. He uses official tradition language: "I received from the Lord what I also passed on to you" (1 Corinthians 11:23 NIV).

From the Last Supper on, the church has celebrated this holy meal. The great reformers Luther, Zwingli, and Calvin never challenged the central place of Holy Communion in the church.

They were reforming what they felt were medieval abuses of this central act of worship.

Even if Zwingli is right, that this meal is a mere memorial with no special sacramental power, this rite bears enormous power. Here, at this Table, we are linked to the church all the way back to the apostles. What we do at the Lord's Table places us in unbroken unity with the historic church and the church around the globe. We are part of something, the church of Christ, that altered history forever. What a heritage and what roots!

The Eternality of the Sacrament

This central place of the sacrament is not the whole story. The Lord's Table bears eternal significance. Zwingli was wrong (I think!). There is more here than a mere memory of Jesus and his work. The language Paul uses indicates the powerful significance of the Lord's Table. This meal is a *koinonia*, Paul argues. There are few more powerful words in Paul's church vocabulary than *koinonia*. Some of you know what that word means. You are in *koinonia* groups. There you share life and faith in order to grow. The word means just that. It's a sharing, a participation in, a partnership concerning. This meal, Paul says, is a sharing in Christ's body and blood.

He doesn't define how that sharing happens or in what mode Christ is present. Regardless of the trajectory of the theological discussion, one thing is clear. Something is going on here! Christ is sharing himself with us in this bread and this cup.

This meal is a covenant, Paul goes on to say. Covenant is one of the biggest words in the Bible. It describes God's fundamental relationship with his people. In a series of covenants, God binds himself irrevocably and eternally to his people. That's what a covenant is—a binding by oath. In fact, God declares that he will cease to exist and the universe will implode before he will break his word to be our God.

This covenant in his blood is about as significant and as spiritually powerful as anything can be. Here God comes to us and binds himself to us, his church. And here we answer God by committing ourselves to Christ and to each other. After all, the church is a covenant between people who make a covenant before God to follow Christ, to be the church.

Paul warns that abuse of this holy meal is a failure to discern the body. Such abuse of Christ's church will be met with discipline, even judgment. God guards this meal carefully, and we should celebrate it expectantly.

The discussion among the churches and theologians is called Real Presence. Is the Lord here, not in imagination and memory, but really here to feed his people? Of course, that can be a dry, even divisive, discussion. But now and then the idea takes on flesh and lives.

Sacramental Reality

Early in my ministry, I lived in an unusual town. The churches in our little village worked together, even worshiped together on occasion. Each Holy Week we conducted ecumenical services. It was ecumenicity in reality. It was natural and not forced.

One year we decided to do the unthinkable. We had a union Communion service. It was difficult, and two of the churches just couldn't join us. Among those who remained, the Lutherans had the largest obstacle. The pastor asked his bishop for permission. He came back with one question: "Do you guys believe in the Real Presence?" We all said yes. He asked no more questions; we offered no more information!

I will never forget it as long as I live. I stood behind the altar rail of the Methodist church with my brothers in ministry. A Lutheran, a Methodist, a Baptist, and a Nazarene served together at the Table of God. God's people came and knelt before us to be fed. They came from all the churches to be fed by all the pastors.

What a night! What power! What presence! Christ was there that night, really there. Walls fell. The church was one. Ministers worked together. The people of God were graced.

I can imagine nothing more powerfully relevant for a world like ours than this meal we call the Lord's Supper. We live in a world emptied of the divine. It is flattened out and soul-less. People and culture have burned themselves out trying to find some meaning in life, some significance on this planet so devoid of anything divine. It leaves many people lost, alone, and longing. We have eaten at all the wrong tables trying to feed our souls, and this world leaves us empty.

What could be more necessary and significant than this meal we eat this day? Someone has come from the other side to help us, to feed our souls. Jesus Christ came from God with God's good news for poor human souls. He left his Spirit. He left his body—the church. In this meal and among his people where his Spirit lives, he comes to feed us. Here is a glimpse of eternity, food for your soul, a touch from God.

David Charles Fisher is pastor of The Colonial Church of Edina, Minneapolis, Minnesota, a Congregational church. Previously pastor of Park Street Church in Boston, he earned his M.Div. degree at Trinity Evangelical Divinity School and his Th.M. and Ph.D. in New Testament studies from Southern Baptist Theological Seminary. He is widely published in magazines and professional journals and is the author of *The 21st-Century Pastor: A Vision Based on the Ministry of Paul* (Grand Rapids: Zondervan, 1996).

16

Thanksgiving and the Cup of Blessing

JOHN H. WHITE

How can I repay the LORD
for all his goodness to me?
I will lift up the cup of salvation
and call on the name of the LORD.
Psalm 116:12–13 NIV

To some who were confident of their own right-eousness and looked down on everybody else, Jesus told this parable: "Two men went up to the temple to pray, one a Pharisee and the other a tax collector. The Pharisee stood up and prayed about himself: 'God, I thank you that I am not like other men—robbers, evildoers, adulterers—or even like this tax collector. I fast twice a week and give a tenth of all I get.' But the tax collector stood at a distance. He would not even look up to heaven, but beat his breast and said, 'God, have mercy on me, a sinner.' I tell you that this man, rather than

the other, went home justified before God. For everyone who exalts himself will be humbled, and he who
humbles himself will be exalted."

Luke 18:9–14 NIV

Communion service is an expression of thanksgiving.
It is often called the Eucharist—giving thanks. That
reality, however, causes challenging questions. How can
I give adequate and acceptable thanksgiving to the Lord of grace,
providence, and glory? Our hearts are often overwhelmed with
the recognition of God's goodness, especially at the time of a
Communion celebration. We reflect on being born into a country of freedom and plenty and, for many of us, the privilege of
birth into believing homes and the experience of God's grace in
Christ. On and on the list could go; even in the midst of diffi-
culties, when we reflect on the experience of God's grace over
against the judgment we justly deserve, thanksgiving floods our
consciousness. Therefore, the question remains: How can we
give adequate and acceptable thanksgiving to the triune God?

Artificial Thanksgiving

The story of the Pharisee and the tax collector provokes even
deeper reflection on our question. Here are two men, one with
thanksgiving on his lips but whose thanksgiving is rejected. The
implication is that such thanksgiving brings an even greater judgment from God.

Therefore, it is vital that we look first at the supposed thanksgiving of the Pharisee. In our ecclesiastical culture, Pharisees
have often been given a bad reputation. One way to express the
strongest derogatory judgment on a fellow church member is to
call him or her a Pharisee. Yet within the culture of the early
church it was far from a derogatory term. Pharisees were good
church members who were in dead earnest about their religion.
They were laymen not preachers, and their sincerity was demonstrated by two things. First, they gave tithes of all that they

107

had. We are told that their scrupulosity included tithing the tiny seasoning leaves of mint, anise, and cumin. In addition, they fasted twice a week.

Here is a man who was willing to sacrifice his pocketbook and his stomach for the sake of religion. Surely such sacrifice demonstrates sincerity. His thanksgiving involved a meticulous attention to the minutia of the Levitical Law and a willingness to go beyond it.

Further, his thanksgiving focused on his contrast to others: "God, I thank you that I am not like other men—robbers, evildoers, adulterers—or even like this tax collector" (Luke 18:11). It sounds like language often used in evangelical circles: "There but for the grace of God go I."

This attitude appears to be one of hearty thanksgiving. In reality, however, it is purely external. Everything that forms the basis of his thanksgiving has to do with external actions. This externality renders his thanksgiving suspect. Jesus, on the other hand, makes it clear that what matters is the heart. God looks on the heart. One day Jesus was accused in the marketplace of breaking God's law by plucking and eating grain on the Sabbath. By way of response, Jesus said, in effect, "It is not what goes into a man that defiles him but what comes out" (Matthew 15:11). When Jesus interprets the law, he stresses that it involves the heart as much as outward action. The biblical word for *heart* refers to the mystic root of our existence, the root of human action, the fount from which the issues of life flow. It is "the wellspring of life" (Proverbs 4:23). God looks on the heart; therefore thanksgiving begins in the heart.

Second, he was filled with self-interest. In the span of two verses, the man used the first person pronoun four times. He was thankful for his own virtue. Thankful that he was a Jew not a Gentile, a Pharisee not a common man. This is not a prayer of thanksgiving but a soliloquy with himself. He was the object of his own insolent self-righteousness.

So the unacceptable nature of his thanksgiving rests on the purely external nature of his actions and the self-centered pride of his life.

Acceptable Thanksgiving

Consider, then, the acceptable thanksgiving of the tax collector. In sharp contrast to the Pharisee, he was a social outcast. He had by his loyalty to the Roman government rejected his ethnic heritage. It is likely that he was both a thief and a cheat and thus a quisling of Rome.

However, even though he never mentions thanksgiving, he had the foundation for acceptable thanksgiving. In contrast to the braggadocio of the Pharisee, he demonstrated his utter humility. He stood far off from the temple. At the temple, the unique presence of God was manifest in the Holy of Holies and in the Shekinah glory. Yet, he dared not draw nigh to such presence. Also, he would not lift his eyes to heaven. There too is the presence of God, but he was so burdened by his sin that he could not look to God. Therefore, he beat on his breast. It is an external expression of the recognition that his problem was internal. The Oriental believed that the breast is the seat of the soul and heart. He did not beat on his brow and thus say my problem is intellectual, but I've been good-hearted. Rather, this action is the expression of a broken spirit, a broken and contrite heart, and leads to his prayer: God, have mercy on me, a sinner.

What did he confess? His sin! He may not have been a murderer, adulterer, or extortioner, but the word *sinner* applied to him. There were no false jewels or pretended virtues. The foundation for his thanksgiving is one plea—being a sinner. His thanksgiving is not based on providential blessing, nor outward actions, and certainly not on his righteousness, but on the confession of sinfulness.

What did he request? God, have mercy on me, a sinner. The actual word translated *mercy* is better translated *propitiated*. It is a biblical word that reminds us that we deserve God's wrath but are objects of his love. It is the same word used in Hebrews 2:17: Jesus is "a merciful and faithful high priest." Clearly such a prayer speaks in anticipation of Jesus Christ and, especially for us in the fullness of the New Testament age, the reality of Christ's substitutionary atonement. Christ is the High Priest who makes expiation for the sins of his people. We are shown that through

Christ's atonement God's wrath is canceled for those trusting in him. This prayer has in view the atonement of Christ. It is not enough merely to plead your sin. The expression of true thanksgiving looks to the cross—to the Lamb of God slain from the foundation of the world.

If you are indeed thankful, you must go to Calvary. If you will give adequate thanks, you must look to the cross. Therefore, the expression of true thanksgiving will be, "Father, I have sinned. Have mercy on me through your Son."

How to Give Thanks

This foundation for and fundamental expression of acceptable thanksgiving is not something new in the Bible; it is also found in Psalm 116. The psalmist reviews the bounty of God's blessings to him, and his heart is bursting with a desire to express thanksgiving. He asks: "How can I repay the LORD for all his goodness to me?" One expects a litany of sacrifices, offerings, and actions—a list of things he will do for God.

The answer, however, is, "I will lift up the cup of salvation and call on the name of the LORD." Give thanks by means of taking something or receiving something? Incredible! Yet, that is precisely what the passage teaches. The acceptable means of thanksgiving is to receive the gospel of grace found in Jesus Christ. The metaphor of this psalm is reenacted in the action steps of the Communion service. As a believer, trusting in Christ alone for your right standing with God, you take the cup of Communion and drink it to the full. The Communion cup is called the cup of blessing (1 Corinthians 10:16 KJV). By symbolic action you receive Christ and embrace his lordship, bringing it into every fiber of your being.

How can you give thanks for food, shelter, health, and the other gifts of his common grace and refuse the greatest gift? At the heart of the Communion service, God is saying to us, "If you are truly thankful for bread, remember: 'Man does not live on bread alone but on every word that comes from the mouth of the LORD'" (Deuteronomy 8:3). We are only truly thankful when we sincerely say through the Communion service, "God, be merciful to me, a sinner." Paul affirms that the cup brings us into fellowship with the blood of Christ (1 Corinthians 10:16). It is the Communion celebration that focuses our attention on the heart of thanksgiving: "Thanks be to God for his indescribable gift!" (2 Corinthians 9:15).

So, therefore, in the name of Christ, I invite you to express the joy of true thanksgiving and recommitment to your salvation by symbolically drinking of the cup of Christ's redemption provided for you by his sovereign grace.

Born in Newburgh, New York, and educated at Geneva College, Reformed Theological Seminary, University of Pittsburgh, and Pittsburgh Theological Seminary, John H. White is president of Geneva College in Beaver Falls, Pennsylvania. A former president of the National Association of Evangelicals and chairman of the board of World Relief, Dr. White is the editor of *The Book of Books* (Phillipsburg, N.J.: Presbyterian and Reformed Publishers, 1978), author of *From Slavery to Servanthood* (Suwannee, Ga.: Great Commission Publications, 1990), and a contributor to other publications. He is a minister in the Reformed Presbyterian Church of North America.

17

Communion: Hard to Understand, Easy to Apply

CHARLES BULLER

> Many of his disciples said, "This is a hard teaching.
> Who can accept it?"
>
> John 6:60 NIV

*I*t is worth asking why John does not make a big deal about the Last Supper in his Gospel story or to consider why he does not spend much time defining the human element of Christ's earthly ministry period. The reason does not require a long explanation. John's ministry was to uphold the absolute divinity of Christ. He and the Holy Spirit selectively pick a lot of stories that emphasize Christ's majesty and his holiness and divine nature.

A Sunday school teacher once asked his class, "What is furry with four legs and loves to gather acorns?" One sharp youngster responded, "I know the answer is supposed to be Jesus, but it sure sounds like a squirrel to me!" Similarly, John was more sophisticated in his analysis but had some proclivity to just want to talk about Jesus' divinity, no matter what the subject matter at hand. This Gospel also celebrates the relational nature of Christ's humanity and why it is important to our salvation.

Communion Demands Attention

Jesus, in the synagogue in Capernaum, had just finished telling the disciples how important it was for them to eat and drink his flesh and blood. Those who do not eat and drink my flesh, he told them, have no life. He went on to make them a promise that he would raise at the last day whoever ate his flesh and drank his blood.

Even the disciples struggled to accept his humanity as part of the equation of our salvation. They raised the question that forms our text: "This is a hard teaching. Who can accept it?"

Anybody who has worked in marketing or sales knows that, regardless of personal ability, slick presentations, or flat-out sales skill, you finally have to live and die with the product you sell. We can never accuse Jesus of selling something he did not deliver or of touching up his approach or slightly altering the product to grab a larger market share. He sold what he was. Usually what he had to sell was not hard to accept, and at other times no one wanted it. For example, the offer of eternal salvation was not a tough sell. "For God so loved the world that he gave his one and only Son, that whoever believes in him shall not perish but have eternal life" (John 3:16) was not a saying hard to accept. Christ said it and then delivered it. The prospect of God's care and watchfulness was certainly a compelling message that is not a hard sell. However, now and again what Jesus had to offer was hard to understand and hard to accept. In such instances, Christ never flinched; he did not alter his message to soften the blow. This text is a prime example of that. So, we do not doubt that had we been there our voices might have joined the chorus of

113

those asking the question: "This is a hard saying. Who can accept it?" That means one of two things.

First, it can mean that it is hard to understand, as math was for me when I was in school. That side of my brain was just challenged. I could study. I could get tutors. I could look at a math problem forever and say, "This is hard; I'm not sure I understand it."

Second, it can mean, "I get it, but I don't like it; I understand it, but I'm not liking what I hear." It is like your accountant asking you on April 15, "Do you understand how much you owe?" We understand all right. We just don't like what we just heard. For example, recently as I was surfing the net for some potential sermon humor, I came across a great joke. I told it to my wife and she laughed with me. Then she added, "You know, the problem, Chuck, is that you can't use that in your sermon. It is not a dirty joke, but it would lower the dignity of your office." So I replied, "I understand what you are saying, but I don't like it. I'm still short one joke."

Sometimes knowing what Jesus said was just hard to accept, for his disciples and for us as well. That is what this text means.

Consider, if you will, what the church has done historically with these words and the words that surround them. Consider, for example, the confusion that this hard saying of Jesus has spawned and the interesting ideas that have grown out of it. In the first century, the church had to fight off the notion that Christians were a cannibalistic bunch. Because they met in living rooms and homes all over the cities, it was not long before the Jewish authorities and Roman government made assumptions about their private cannibalistic ceremonies and ostracized them. It took a while to live down that rumor.

In the second century, the Christian Gnostics, that day's version of the New Age movement, taught that you could pretty much ignore your flesh, because it was your spirit that saved you. John 6:63 was a favorite: "The Spirit gives life; the flesh counts for nothing." You could revel in your flesh and live it up, or you could be an ascetic monk and deny your flesh. You could do whatever you wanted with your flesh. It did not matter. It was your spirit that got you saved. It took a long time for the church to come out of that. Indeed, it is still part of the so-called "health and wealth gospel." There is a sense in which we are not yet out of it.

About the ninth century, the church developed a theory called transubstantiation, which is still part of Roman Catholicism. It teaches that, in the Communion elements, the bread and wine actually become the body and blood of our Lord Jesus Christ. This text would be useful in that theology. This theory and others around the Lord's Supper serve to show us that it has always grabbed the attention of believers and unbelievers alike.

Communion Declares My Freedom and God's Tugging

Communion raises an interesting question: Why did God permit his Word to be written in such a way that Christians could have amazingly different opinions about this important aspect of the life of the church? Why did he not simply spell it out in ten steps and stop right there? The answer is not very complicated; it is because he too much respects our freedom. At the heart of salvation and at the heart of what Communion symbolizes is that we have freedom to partake and freedom to ignore this celebration. Our ability to understand God and respond to him only has real meaning if we have the ability to misunderstand him also. That is the ultimate tribute of our freedom in Christ. It shows how much God respects the fact that we are free moral beings.

A young man, a friend of mine, grew up in the church. He rarely, if ever, missed a service. God was always a part of his life in a unique way. When we were younger, he often told me how this made him doubt the authenticity of his faith. I wish now that I could go back and tell him that the right answer to his concern is in Communion. I wish I had said to him, "Do you understand that to continue to choose to believe is the ultimate tribute that God pays to you in this event?" We choose, unlike the disciples on the day of the cross, not to walk away, saying, "This is too hard."

In Communion we not only remember that Christ died but that we are called to pick up our cross and follow him. We celebrate the mystery of this event, how God uses these elements of bread and wine to confirm our faith and salvation. John 6:66 is still a valid option for us: "Many of his disciples turned back and no longer followed him." They said, "I'm out of here. I didn't think it was going to be this hard." Others, however, were with Peter who said, in effect, "I'll tell you what, Lord. That is hard to understand sometimes, but where else can we go? You alone have the words of eternal life" (see John 6:68).

It boils down to this: Either the body and blood of Christ is the only source of true living, or it is not. Here at the Lord's Table we proclaim our exclusive hope in the body and blood of our Lord Jesus Christ.

I am convinced that the number one issue for Christians in the next century will be the exclusive claim of Christ that he was the one and only Bread of Life. There may be no other ideology, no other ground, on which the church fights its most serious battles than this one right here. It is a hard saying, that only in Christ can you eat his flesh and drink his blood and have eternal life, that his Spirit is the only Spirit that gives life. Many will hear that message; some will grow up with the very things of Christ and say, "I'm sorry, it is just too hard for me." The fact will be the same, unless there is that Holy Spirit enabling at some point and you walk away and say, "No more. It is too hard." Communion is a reminder that God has allowed us to make that choice and, compelled by his Spirit, to find in his body and his flesh all that creates eternal life.

I think of Perry, a previously agnostic friend. He had doubts because he was a bit afraid of what he did not know. He announced one day that he had decided to give his life to Christ. I asked, "Why?" He said, "I am convinced." He was very scientific in his outlook and added, "I think I finally understood that this other power, a dark force, was using evolution as a smoke screen to keep me away from life that is truly free in Christ. So, I have given my life to him." Perry was caught in a tug between God and Satan and finally, freely, gave his life to Jesus.

Communion Invites Commitment

In the late 1800s, there was an English preacher by the name of Charles Barry. Once a pastor in London, he later became the pastor of the great Plymouth Church in Brooklyn. Later in his life, out of honest reflection, Barry related how he had come to Christ: There had been a time, early in his ministry, when he preached what he later called "a very thin gospel." He looked upon Jesus as a great teacher, a wonderful communicator, a nice guy; but he underestimated his claim to be the only bread that gives life. Late one night during his first pastorate, as Barry sat in his cozy little study, he heard a knock at the door. He opened the door and standing before him saw a girl with a shawl over her shoulders. She asked, "Are you a minister?" He replied, "Yes, I am." She responded, "You must come with me. I want to get my mother in." Assuming her to be the daughter of some drunken woman, Barry said, "You have the wrong person. You need to go to the police." She pleaded, "No, my mother is dying. You must come and get her into heaven."

Barry dressed quickly and followed the young woman for a mile or more through the cold, dark, lonely streets of London to a room in a run-down neighborhood. He kneeled at the sick woman's bedside and told her about a good and kind Savior called Jesus who would be on the other side to greet her when she died. The weak but desperate woman cut him off with her words, "But, mister, look. That's no use for me. I'm a sinner. I've lived my life away from God. Can you tell me about someone who can save my soul?" Barry said later, "I stood there in the presence of a dying woman and realized I had nothing to tell her. In the midst of her sin and death, I had no message that would help. In order to give something to that dying woman, I leaped back in memory to my mother's knee, my cradle of faith. I told her the story of the cross and of a Christ who is able to save. Tears ran down her cheeks and she said, 'Mister, now you're getting it. Now you're getting me in.'" Barry concluded, "I got her in and, thanks be to God, I got myself in too."

For all of us who are believers, who have asked Christ into our lives, Communion is our dramatization that God in Christ has gotten us in. He is the only Bread of Life, and his is the only blood that cleanses us from all sin. For all of the confusion that flows from this text, and for all the debates the church has had, the bread and wine contain a very simple meaning: God has placed on Jesus the penalty for our sin. He has taken that sin away from us through his broken body and shed blood. Communion reminds us that our decision to follow Christ has been made real by a cross on Calvary. He has gotten us in!

Charles Buller pastors Neighborhood Mennonite Brethren Church in Visalia, California. He is chairman of Mission USA of the Mennonite Brethren Church Planting and Renewal Commission and was previously board chairman for Mennonite Brethren Biblical Seminary in Fresno, California. He earned his B.S. degree at Fresno Pacific University and his M.Div. from Mennonite Brethren Biblical Seminary.

18

The Kingdom of God Is like a Family . . .

CARL C. FICKENSCHER II

(Jesus) was saying, "The kingdom of God is like a man who casts seed upon the soil; and goes to bed at night and gets up by day, and the seed sprouts up and grows—how, he himself does not know. The soil produces crops by itself; first the blade, then the head, then the mature grain in the head. But when the crop permits, he immediately puts in the sickle, because the harvest has come." And He said, "How shall we picture the kingdom of God, or by what parable shall we present it? It is like a mustard seed, which, when sown upon the soil, though it is smaller than all the seeds that are upon the soil, yet when it is sown, grows up and becomes larger than all the garden plants and forms large branches; so that the birds of the air can nest under its shade." And with many such parables He was speaking the word to them as they were able to hear it; and He did not speak to them without a parable; but He was explaining everything privately to His own disciples.

Mark 4:26–34 NASB

*T*he kingdom of God is like a father who held his new daughter in his arms. She was so tiny, so helpless. On this night, she wasn't quite ready for sleep. He rocked and she cried, and he rocked and she cried, and he rocked and she cried some more, until, finally, he laid her in her crib, and he lay down to sleep too.

When he woke up, he was amazed. She wasn't a baby anymore. It was just as everyone had said: "They grow up before you know it." She was a woman, married, with a family of her own. Suddenly, just as if it had been overnight, the man was left with only the photo albums and the memories. So he rocked and he sighed, and he rocked and he sighed, and he rocked and he sighed some more, until, finally, he opened the album and began to reminisce.

Oh, she was a beautiful baby. Her eyes closed so tight. So trusting. So innocent. Well, not innocent, really. He remembered those words he'd heard so often in church: "Little children, though seemingly innocent, are by birth and nature sinful. . . . All men from the fall of Adam are conceived and born in sin and so are under the wrath of God and would be lost forever unless delivered by our Lord Jesus Christ." That's why they'd brought their daughter to be baptized. See—wasn't she adorable in her little white gown? A lovely symbol, wasn't it? White, the way in baptism the Holy Spirit had washed her clean of all her sins, made her as holy as Christ himself.

A couple of years later, their son had worn the same gown. Dad wasn't too crazy about that—"My boy in a dress? Oh, I guess it's OK this time. It's the water with the Word that matters." The man chuckled now as he remembered.

"Look at this one, sweetheart," he said to his wife, who was rocking in the chair next to him. In this photo all the kids were lined up on the couch. Their youngest was mugging for the camera. Their eldest—let's see, she must be about seven here—was looking quite the little lady. "Honey, remember how we always used to sit on that couch for our family devotions?"

"In your dreams, dear. I'm not sure there was ever a night when they all sat."

"Oh, I know. But they all listened. Remember how much they'd surprise us? We would think they hadn't heard a word, and then when we got to the 'Let's Think It Over' questions, they knew exactly what the story was about."

"Yeah, and they loved to sing. That was your favorite part."

"Un-huh. All the Jesus songs."

They turned to pictures of camping trips and Halloween costumes and Christmases. And here was confirmation day. Again, quite the lady. Except this time, she almost did look like a lady. Her hair all fixed. Wearing heels. And, again, wearing white. Thirteen years later, the same white of her baptism. Still washed in the blood of Christ. Still forgiven by Jesus' cross. Same faith in the Savior. Not quite as childlike, not quite as perfect as at her baptism, but the same faith. And, in a sense, it had grown. Deeper understanding. The things she'd always believed she could fit together more clearly now. You could see how God's Word had been working on her—oh, not in the picture but in her life. She'd asked great questions—like why God made us if he knew Jesus would have to die to bail us out. And you could see that the answers made her appreciate God's love even more. She'd worked hard in those confirmation classes—learning her memory assignments, reviewing for the examination.

Here she was at a piano recital. Fifteen. Still couldn't drive herself. JV basketball team. Choir. Drama club.

"She was fabulous in *My Fair Lady*," the man mused.

"You were so proud of her."

"You bet I was!"

"You only wished you could have been up there with her, playing Professor 'enry 'iggins."

"Daddy always wants to be his little girl's man. Look. Here she is on her first date. First car date. Glad she waited as long as she did for that."

"We worried a little, didn't we?"

"Not so much that she'd do something sinful. We always trusted her. Just that she'd finally choose someone who would really build her up in her faith. Someone who believed in Jesus as beautifully as she did."

"Did I ever tell you what she told me about that once?"

"I don't think so."

121

"Well, one time we were having girl talk. This was when she was out of school, working. And she was wondering if she'd ever meet the right guy. She was worried about it too—different from the way we were worried; she wasn't sure anyone would come along."

"Yeah, right, as darling as she was."

"Oh, I know. But she was worried about it. And she said that's when Holy Communion really became special to her."

"No kidding. How come?"

"Because she said every night she'd pray that God would help her find the right man—active in his faith like she was—and then, when she'd kneel at the Communion rail, God would answer. He'd give her just the right man: Jesus. Right there in the flesh. Then she always knew she had *him*. And if she had him, then everything else would work out fine. Plus, she said, she also knew she had forgiveness for thinking the wrong things about guys sometimes."

"I didn't know girls thought those things."

The next set of pictures, a whole lot of them, confirmed how beautifully God does answer prayers. Daddy's little girl wearing white again. Standing with her the very man who shared her faith, who loved Jesus in the very same way she did. He would make a wonderful husband, a sweet daddy. He would give Daddy's grown-up girl a very happy life, with babies and baptisms and family devotions and confirmations. Maybe before long Grandpa would even see some more weddings.

He closed the photo album and rocked back in his chair. There'd been a time when he'd been one alone. Then he'd become two. Then three. Now many. It seemed he'd just gone to sleep one night, his baby daughter laid in the crib, and now he was the patriarch of a whole clan.

"It sure has worked out beautifully, hasn't it, sweetheart?"

"What has?"

"Our life, our family. How did they all turn out so well? We sure didn't do anything special."

The farmer in today's text didn't do anything special either. Our text is not specifically about fathers and families, although they certainly may be included. The seed, the crops, the trees, like the father and his family, are just illustrations, parables. Jesus is talking about the kingdom of God.

Nevertheless, the message of the parables—the two in the text and the one in our sermon—is the same. It is that the kingdom of God grows in much the same way as a seed and in the very same way as a Christian family. It happens virtually without our noticing . . . and with God doing all the real work. With seed, he does it by water and sunshine. With the kingdom—as with Christian families—he does it by his means of grace: baptism, Holy Communion, his Word.

Sometimes the growth seems so insignificant, you hardly notice. You really wonder if anybody's listening. You wonder what good the Word is really doing. It certainly seems as if baptizing our babies, receiving Christ's body and blood, are doing nothing special at all. Of course it seems that way, because those we can see doing something—pastor, parents, communicants— aren't doing anything special.

Just as great things happen while the farmer sleeps, as fathers and mothers go about their most ordinary parental routines, so God is doing great things invisibly through his Word and sacraments. Our children are hearing; the Holy Spirit is working in their hearts. The world is being reached; sins are being forgiven; souls are being won for eternity. Every day, every minute, God's Word is bringing the increase.

Perhaps not until heaven, but one of these days we'll look around us and see that the kingdom has grown into a great clan, with people from every nation under heaven; people we've never met and people very, very close to us. One of these days we'll wake up and see what great things God's Word and sacraments have done.

"How did they all turn out so well? We sure didn't do anything special."

"No, dear, we didn't."

Born in San Mateo, California, Carl C. Fickenscher II holds a Ph.D. in homiletics from Southwestern Baptist Theological Seminary. He earned his M.Div. from Concordia Theological Seminary. In addition to being pastor of Peace Lutheran Church (Missouri Synod) in Garland, Texas, he is an adjunct professor at Concordia Seminary and is published by Concordia Press.

19

Growing Principles from the Head Gardener's Son

PAUL E. ENGLE

I am the true vine, and my Father is the gardener. He cuts off every branch in me that bears no fruit, while every branch that does bear fruit he prunes so that it will be even more fruitful. You are already clean because of the word I have spoken to you. Remain in me, and I will remain in you. No branch can bear fruit by itself; it must remain in the vine. Neither can you bear fruit unless you remain in me. I am the vine; you are the branches. If a man remains in me and I in him, he will bear much fruit; apart from me you can do nothing. If anyone does not remain in me, he is like a branch that is thrown away and withers; such branches are picked up, thrown into the fire and burned. If you remain in me and my words remain in you, ask whatever you wish, and it will be given you. This is to my Father's glory, that you bear much fruit, showing yourselves to be my disciples.

John 15:1–8 NIV

I s the family dinner table becoming a dinosaur? Americans are spending a growing amount of money on eating out. Two-career marriages, children with after-school sports and music lessons, as well as other time pressures on family members mean that the cozy 1950s scene of mother, father, and two children engaged in animated conversation as they enjoy a meal together is becoming increasingly rare. Is the decline of the family dinner scene a bad omen for the future of the family? Opinions differ.

Neglect of another kind of family meal, however, is most certainly to our detriment. On the evening before his execution, Christ gathered his close friends together for a final meal that would be known forever as the Last Supper.

Do you remember the events of that historic night? All twelve disciples huddled together with Jesus over a Passover meal. As they did, one dissenting disciple slipped off into the darkness while the meal was still in progress. Christ continued to talk to his remaining disciples. Suddenly, he commanded, "Come, now; let us leave" (John 14:31).

They all stood up to leave the room. One by one they descended the stairs and walked through the dark city streets toward the Garden of Gethsemane, where Christ received the bitter Judas kiss. Somewhere on the way to that kiss Christ spoke the words recorded in John 15. A careful study reveals the central focus of his teaching.

We Must Remain in Christ

The word *remain*, which is repeated eight times in this passage, denotes a key concept. Christ's repetition indicates its importance. He further reinforces his teaching through an analogy from the world of viticulture: I am the true vine and my Father is the gardener.

The disciples understood. Grapevines were a common sight around Jerusalem. The coins of the Maccabees bore the engraving of a vine. The temple gates were adorned with carved vines and grape clusters. Vineyards covered many hillsides outside the city. Some scholars suggest that Christ was passing through one of the vineyards when he made these remarks. Imagine him holding up a thick vine heavy with the weight of ripening grapes as he declared, "I am the true vine."

The Old Testament, which his listeners had heard in the temple, compares Israel to a vine. Hosea 10:1 says, "Israel is a luxuriant vine" (NRSV). Jeremiah 2:21 says, "I planted you as a choice vine, from the purest stock" (NRSV). Now Christ claims that he is Israel's authentic Vine and they must remain in him.

What does it mean to remain in the True Vine? The equation is this: A branch is to the vine as a believer is to Christ. To remain in Christ means joining him in a living, continuous, growing way. It means refusing to allow sin to hinder our relationship with him. It means acknowledging our utter dependence on him for, "Apart from me," he says, "you can do nothing" (John 15:5 NIV).

To abide in Christ means we look to him for wisdom with our work, our family responsibilities, our finances, our social life, and whatever else we do. Christ wants us to retain daily fellowship with him in every room of our lives. By doing so, we become productive persons.

We Need to Produce Fruit

We were born for a purpose and that purpose is to bear fruit for Christ. Our lives will be productive only if we are true branches rather than false ones. False branches are the disappointing ones that fail to produce fruit. Christ says he cuts off every branch that bears no fruit: "If anyone does not remain in me, he is like a branch that is thrown away and withers; such branches are picked up, thrown into the fire and burned" (John 15:6 NIV).

Christ warned about the danger of barren branches. His warning identified someone fresh on the disciples' minds: Judas, the traitor. Judas, by his heinous act, failed Christ's vine test. His fruit was so bitter that even today we speak of betrayal as a Judas kiss. Apparently his connection to Christ was never more than one of external, surface appearance. Today we might call him a culture Christian.

Fruitless branches are no good. They are dead wood, good only for the fire. This sobering warning arrests us about the dangers of shallow, counterfeit Christianity. Not all who attend Christian churches or mouth words are genuine.

What sort of fruit do we exhibit? If you looked up the word *fruit* in a concordance, you would find that the Bible uses it to refer to productive, godly character traits. For example, Isaiah 5:7 says God is looking for the fruit of justice and righteousness. Galatians 5:22–23 talks about the fruit of love, joy, peace, patience, kindness, goodness, faithfulness, gentleness, and self-control. This is the fruit Christ expects to be hanging from the branches of each of our lives. It demonstrates that Christ is the source of life in us.

As we digest Christ's teaching on this subject, we can draw conclusions. For one thing, fruit bearing cannot be simulated. Have you ever spotted a bowl of delicious looking fruit on the other side of a room, and your mouth salivates in anticipation of the first bite of a succulent pear or peach? Then you make your way across the room toward the bowl only to find disappointment. A closer examination reveals that the enticing object is nothing more than a plastic imitation. No matter how attractive simulated fruit may look from a distance, it cannot compare with the real thing. It will never feed you.

Likewise, the fruit that Christ expects in our life cannot be simulated by human efforts. We produce true fruit only as we depend upon him, for Christ says, "No branch can bear fruit by itself; it must remain in the vine. Neither can you bear fruit unless you remain in me" (John 15:4 NIV).

Now he speaks of the Holy Spirit's fruit in us. If patience is missing, or joy is incomplete, or self-control is absent, or some other fruit of the Spirit is lacking, we can acquire it only by remaining close to Christ. We will find it only in his strength. There are no other options, no substitutes, no shortcuts to bearing fruit. We are either growing in Christ or we are dead wood.

A further conclusion to be drawn from this text is that true fruit bearing, though never simulated, can be stimulated. We can

127

arouse the Spirit's work in us. Paul tells Timothy to "Stir up the gift of God which is in you" (2 Timothy 1:6 NKJV).

Some years ago, I planted some vickery bushes in the yard of my suburban Chicago home. After the first growing season, I neglected to prune them back. When the plants finally started growing again the following season, they were quite pathetic looking. Somewhat belatedly, I pruned them again, this time almost to the ground. My close cropped pruning stimulated growth, amazing growth. Indeed, the astounding growth of my once severely pruned vickery bushes became the talk of our neighborhood.

That is precisely what God does in us. He watches over us and, as he sees the need, determines to do some pruning. Pruning can be painful. When we are pruned of health, or job, or some valued possessions, or worldly security, there is almost always discomfort involved. How tempting it can be, at such times, to throw in the towel, to wring our hands in despair, or to entertain bitter thoughts toward God, as Job's wife did.

We do well to remember that God's pruning knife is always in safe hands. It is in hands that are always loving, wise, and good. He never prunes us randomly or carelessly. He plans every cut and prunes us carefully to make us more fruitful to fulfill the master plan for our life.

Perhaps you have been through his pruning process. Perhaps you are going through it now. Hold on, little branch. Remember him who skillfully wields the knife. You will come out better than you ever were before when his work is accomplished.

Fruit bearing also leads to effective prayers: "If you remain in me and my words remain in you, ask whatever you wish, and it will be given you." What an encouraging promise to motivate us to prayer!

Does it mean that all prayers find answers? No, it does not. Note the qualifications in the text. We must maintain an unbroken connection with Christ. The psalmist reminds us, "If I regard iniquity in my heart, the Lord will not hear me" (Psalm 66:18 KJV). When we remain in Christ, we are more apt to ask for those things that are in line with God's will, rather than self-centered requests.

There is a condition attached to having an effective prayer life and having Christ's words remain in us. The condition is that we need to be familiar with his words and practice them. Let us not then be heard among the chorus of those who waste their breath praying for things that openly contradict Scripture. A fruitful Christian is saturated with, and shaped by, Scripture in his daily prayers.

Another characteristic of our fruit bearing is that it glorifies our heavenly Father. When a healthy, productive garden or a beautiful fruit orchard catches your eye, your inclination is to commend the gardener and not the fruit. Likewise, if we develop the fruit of Christlike qualities in our lives, they will reflect well on the heavenly Gardener.

A final characteristic of fruit bearing is that it will serve as a verification of discipleship. Christ said, "You bear much fruit, showing yourselves to be my disciples" (John 15:8). He also taught in Matthew 7, "By their fruit you will recognize them." Ultimately God alone judges the genuineness of each person's faith. However, a complete absence of fruit in a life should call into question whether a person is truly connected to the True Vine. A verbal profession of belief in Christ rings a rather hollow tone when there is no difference between the person making it and the average Joe or Jane Pagan. A genuine profession, on the other hand, declares that Christ makes a positive difference.

Judas had abruptly disappeared, intent on carrying out his final act of betrayal. Peter would deny Christ in a matter of hours. The other disciples would desert him. No wonder these John 15 words weighed heavily on Christ's heart! The exhortation to remain in him could not have been spoken at a more poignant moment. Do you know someone who once professed to follow Christ yet today is far from him? It can happen to any of us. How can we be certain that we will still be living in a close relationship with Christ a year from now? Five years from now? On our last day?

Practical Steps for Bearing Fruit

What are some practical steps we can take to insure that we continue to remain or abide in Christ over the long haul? The text tells us. The key word is *remain*. That is, be constant; be

129

consistent. Remain constant in prayer. Remain consistent in feeding on the words of Scripture. Be regular at the Lord's Table, for it is for us a means of grace that allows us to renew our commitment to Christ.

You and I must come to grips with the fact that remaining in Christ is a lifelong challenge. It is achievable only through vigorous spiritual discipline and determination.

How are we doing? Are we ever tempted to betray him like Judas? To disown him like Peter? To run away like the others? May that never be so! It will not be so, so long as we remain.

C. S. Lewis made this observation: "Make sure that, if you have once accepted Christianity, then some of its main doctrines shall be deliberately held before your mind for some time every day. That is why daily prayer and religious reading and churchgoing are necessary parts of the Christian life. We have to be continually reminded of what we believe. Neither this belief nor any other will automatically remain alive in the mind. It must be fed. And as a matter of fact, if you examined a hundred people who had lost their faith in Christianity, I wonder how many of them would turn out to have been reasoned out of it by honest argument? Do not most people simply drift away?" (*Mere Christianity* [New York: Macmillan, 1952], 109). Could it happen to you or me? By God's grace, let us who are in union with Christ purpose to be faithful till death to the One in whom it is our highest calling to abide. May our communion around his Table prepare us to bear fruit to the praise and glory of the heavenly Gardener.

Paul E. Engle, a minister in the Presbyterian Church in America, graduated from Houghton College and Wheaton College Graduate School before completing his doctoral studies at Westminster Theological Seminary. He served churches in Pennsylvania, Connecticut, Illinois, and Michigan, before joining Baker Book House Company as Acquisitions Editor of Professional Books and Bibles. He is an author and visiting faculty member at Reformed Theological Seminary and Knox Theological Seminary. His recent books include *Baker's Worship Handbook, Baker's Wedding Handbook,* and *Baker's Funeral Handbook.*

20

Self-Examination

CALVIN B. HANSON

Be imitators of God, therefore, as dearly loved children and live a life of love, just as Christ loved us and gave himself up for us as a fragrant offering and sacrifice to God. But among you there must not be even a hint of sexual immorality, or of any kind of impurity, or of greed, because these are improper for God's holy people. Nor should there be obscenity, foolish talk or coarse joking, which are out of place, but rather thanksgiving. For of this you can be sure: No immoral, impure or greedy person—such a man is an idolater—has any inheritance in the kingdom of Christ and of God. . . . Have nothing to do with the fruitless deeds of darkness, but rather expose them. For it is shameful even to mention what the disobedient do in secret. But everything exposed by the light becomes visible, for it is light that makes everything visible. This is why it is said:

> Wake up, O sleeper,
> rise from the dead,
> and Christ will shine on you.

Be very careful, then, how you live—not as unwise but as wise, making the most of every opportunity, because the days are evil.

Ephesians 5:1–5; 11–16 NIV

*Y*ears ago, as a missionary in Japan, I occasionally stopped by the potters' quarter in the city of Kyoto where we lived. One day I was invited into the inner sanctum of a shop that created exquisite gifts for foreign dignitaries, diplomats, and heads of state on behalf of the Emperor of Japan. Here I found the master potter, a venerable old man with a flowing beard, seated on the *tatami* floor before a low, simple table. His legs were tucked under him. As an assistant placed a piece of delicate pottery into the potter's ancient hands, he would hold it to the light. If the rays revealed even the slightest imperfection, into the waste box it went. Conversely, if the piece passed the test, he then tapped it with a metal rod to check the ring. Only if the ring was right, absolutely true, was the piece inscribed with his own stamp. His stamp signified that he, the master craftsman, had found it to be without flaw or fault, and it was ready for distribution.

This is something of the flavor of the word *examine,* which forms the backdrop to Ephesians 5, and which is foundational to coming to the Lord's Table: "A man ought to examine himself before he eats of the bread and drinks of the cup" (1 Corinthians 11:28 NIV). Believers are to engage in rigorous self-examination, rejoicing in the work of Christ but repenting of that which fails the test.

To understand the scope of meaning of the word *examine,* the participle, *testing,* or *finding out,* must be placed in relation to its context. Some of the more recent translations bracket Ephesians 5 verse 9, which is helpful since this participle in verse 10 modifies the last verb, *live,* in verse 8. Reading it this way gives the full impact of the participle, and so a free translation becomes, in effect, "As children of light walk testing what is pleasing to the Lord." It is important to see that Paul uses *testing* as prescriptive of how the believer is to be walking. The Christian's walk should be characterized continually by an attitude of testing and probing.

The call to earnest examination in regard to the Lord's Table is strengthened further by an exegetical choice in relation to which word the negative clause, "not as fools but as wise" is spoken to in verse 15. Most translations link it to the verb *live* that runs through the passage.

"Don't examine as fools do!" Paul exclaims. How do fools examine? Our text gives a good hint in verse 16 with the phrase "The days are evil." "When in Rome do as the Romans do" is not an acceptable standard for God's people. That, in a sense, was what the Protestant Reformation was about. We are God's people. We do not just go along with the crowd.

The text suggests three tests that the Christian should exercise in coming to the Communion Table and three stamps of approval that accrue as a result of faithful probing in these areas.

Fit for God

The first test is that we examine our walk by what pleases the Lord. This is not only the most important test intrinsically but also structurally, in that this test subsumes the others.

Here is the bold suggestion of the possibility of pleasing the Lord! The force is even stronger than the English word conveys. It is the compound word, *well-pleasing*. Discover not only what pleases the Lord but what pleases him most. Make him well pleased.

When even peers are hard to please, the awesome prospect of pleasing the Almighty seems too much for us. Nevertheless, Scripture affirms this possibility in the example of Enoch, who was commended as one who pleased God (see Hebrews 11:5). Enoch, a man of like passions as we, pleased God well. So can we!

The author of Hebrews uses the verb two more times. This second occurrence gives the prerequisite to pleasing God: "Without faith it is impossible to please him."

When the apostle Paul refers to eating and drinking "unworthily" at the Lord's Table (see 1 Corinthians 11:27), first and foremost he is asking us to examine ourselves to make absolutely certain that we are in the faith.

In ourselves we can never be worthy. We approach the Table with faith in the sufficiency of our Lord's sacrifice and the assurance that we have been made worthy because of the righteousness of our Lord imputed to the believer.

The final occurrence of the verb speaks directly to the thrust of our text as it focuses on the progression in pleasing God: "Do

133

not forget to do good and to share with others, for with such sacrifices God is pleased" (Hebrews 13:16). Clearly, pleasing God
well cannot be a once-for-all exhibition of faith. It is the continual doing good and sharing that pleases God most.

Thus, the first test is to discover or discern what is pleasing
to the Lord. The first stamp of approval we seek comes from the
Lord himself in response to our obedience.

Fit for Fellowship

The second test examines our walk by what is fitting in the
fellowship of believers: "Among you there must not be even a
hint of sexual immorality, or of any kind of impurity, or of greed,
because these are improper for God's holy people" (Ephesians
5:3). Now Paul speaks of the reformation of the human soul.

The Greek text states the principle both positively ("these are
improper for God's holy people," v. 3) and negatively ("what are
not fitting," v. 4). What is fitting or appropriate to the fellowship of the believers must be understood here.

The immediate reference in both verses is to three sins listed,
but the principle "as is fitting for the saints" lifts us into a larger
sphere. This is the same principle Paul illustrates in writing to
the Corinthians. There he says that while eating meat is morally
neutral, in some circumstances and cultures it might not be
appropriate in relation to the saints. In such a setting, it should
be shunned. Here is shifting ground, a principle to be applied to
varying situations. Here testing how we walk is crucial!

In all of this testing we are to take into consideration the whole
fellowship, the church. Sometimes this testing is easier: "For of
this you can be sure: No immoral, impure or greedy person—such
a man is an idolater—has any inheritance in the kingdom of Christ
and of God" (Ephesians 5:5).

Immorality! Impurity! Greed! These prohibitions are glaring
and emphatic. Just previous to this Paul prescribes testing that
becomes a bit sticky: "Nor should there be obscenity, foolish talk
or coarse joking, which are out of place, but rather thanksgiving"
(v. 4).

While the second test of our walk is that it be fitting in the fellowship, the stamp of approval now comes to the individual from the fellowship of believers. Apelles, among those greeted by Paul in his letter to Rome, is an example of one tested and "approved in Christ" (Romans 16:10). The word *approved* has the same stem as the participle *testing* discussed earlier. The full force of the approbation is that Apelles was carefully tested and examined by the fellowship before the seal of approval was placed upon him.

Fit for the Table

The third test is to examine our walk by our own unique need and circumstance. "Be very careful, then, how you live—not as unwise but as wise" (Ephesians 5:15). "A man ought to examine himself before he eats of the bread and drinks of the cup" (1 Corinthians 11:28). Note how intimately these texts ask us to test. Literally, "You examine how you live." It is always a temptation to apply tests to the needs and circumstances of others rather than to ourselves.

With this in mind, come back to the three sins linked together: immorality, impurity, covetousness. It is very easy to let these wash over us. We decry the fact that our times are indeed uniquely evil. We wail over pornography, prostitution, homosexuality, and adultery. We lament the sins of others as we quietly hang out the "Do Not Disturb" sign on the doorknobs of our own lives. Granted that while for some believers sexual sin is an area of acute temptation, most of us can glibly shrug our shoulders and walk away from this part of the text, albeit feeling pained about these evils while smug about ourselves.

While hiking a nature trail, I happened upon a young lad just as he let out a bloodcurdling shriek. He had stuck his hand into a stinging nettle bush! Each leaf of the nettle sustains 10,000 miniature hypodermic needles capable of injecting a painful poison under the skin. Some texts of Scripture are like the stinging nettle, if one looks carefully. The apostle Peter in his first Epistle has a similar text that stings if applied aright: "Abstain from sinful desires, which war against your soul" (1 Peter 2:11).

In the original text a different connective is used, thus encouraging some commentators to construe this meaning. However, this connective is used exclusively to link all three words in Ephesians 5:5. Even more important, the same phrase, "covetousness, which is idolatry," occurs in Colossians 3:5 (KJV), where clearly it is not to be understood in a sexual sense.

Here it is *fleshly lusts*. Sexual sins, again, we say, but it's not our problem. No? The term *sinful desires* is used just this once by Peter, but Paul uses it six times. In two of these it must be something quite different. It must mean material things. In another instance or two it may well mean the same. The "fleshly lust" that wars against the soul just might be the quest to accumulate material things: the "covetousness, which is idolatry" of our Ephesians 5 text.

No, we cannot let ourselves off the hook! Any and all kinds of covetousness, not only those linked with abhorrent sexual transgressions, are thus equated with idolatry. Just as the pain of the stinging nettle fades and passes within a half hour, so also there is danger that the sting of the biblical text can also pass that quickly. Dramatically increasing church budgets, better facilities, and additional ministerial staff (what a friend of mine terms "staff infection") may be a healthy sign. They may also be evidence of the "covetousness, which is idolatry" unless they represent a congregation's commitment to reach the community.

The third test is an honest evaluation of our own needs and circumstances and the attestation is the seal of a clear conscience.

Three tests, three attestations, but only the first one is definitive: that which pleases the Lord! We may, you see, enjoy a clear conscience simply because it is poorly trained. We may enjoy the approval of the local fellowship because they know us for something other than what we really are, or because the standard of the fellowship is less than biblical. While the other tests and affirmations are important, in the final analysis only the test of what pleases God and receives the seal of his approval is definitive!

Some years ago I conducted the funeral for my father-in-law, who in his later years was known quite widely as the "clock-maker."

One of his grandfather clocks, each handcrafted by him from raw boards to finished product with no two exactly alike, was his pride and joy and stood in the dining room in his own home. This clock he had made entirely from wood; not only the case but also the works, except for the sand in the wood cylinder weights. Every single part, from cogs to wheels to face and hands, was fashioned meticulously from wood, and the clock kept perfect time.

Only after the funeral did we find in his basement a large cardboard box filled with parts of sundry sorts and sizes—imperfect pieces that had to be discarded in order for the clock to keep perfect time and merit the seal on the back: "Handcrafted by Art Wessman."

The desire of the Father's heart is that we his children so walk that when the final measure of life is taken he can write over our lives: Handcrafted by the Living God.

Our good God has given us the Lord's Table to help us in this process of self-examination: A man ought to examine himself before he eats of the bread and drinks of the cup. Let us so come to the Communion Table, having applied to our hearts the tests of the Scriptures. May his Spirit bear witness with ours that we have the seal of God's approval upon our lives!

Calvin B. Hanson, a minister in the Evangelical Free Church, was for ten years a missionary to Japan. He was the founding president of Trinity Western College in Langley, British Columbia, Canada. In addition to serving as a pastor in Canada and the United States, he served on the faculty at Trinity Evangelical Divinity School in Deerfield, Illinois. A prolific author, his books include *What It Means to Be Free* (Minneapolis: Free Church Press, 1988), and *Pure Joy* (Langley, B.C.: Trinity Western Press, 1985).

Richard Allen Bodey taught on the faculties of Trinity Evangelical Divinity School in Deerfield, Illinois, and Reformed Theological Seminary in Jackson, Mississippi. He previously served in six Presbyterian pastorates. He is contributing editor of *Good News for All Seasons, Inside the Sermon, The Voice from the Cross,* and *If I Had Only One Sermon to Preach.* Dr. Bodey holds graduate degrees from Princeton Theological Seminary, Westminster Theological Seminary, and Trinity Evangelical Divinity School.

Robert Leslie Holmes has held pastorates in California, Florida, Georgia, and Mississippi. He currently serves as minister of the First Presbyterian Church of Pittsburgh, Pennsylvania. Through the media ministry of that church he is heard across the United States weekly. He is the author of *Don't Try to Stop on a Mountaintop.* Dr. Holmes holds degrees from the University of Mobile (Alabama), Reformed Theological Seminary, and Columbia Theological Seminary.